W9-AYE-228

PROPERTY OF:
KENTLAKE HIGH SCHOOL LIBRARY

WORLD
HISTORY SERIES ▪▪▪

Women's Suffrage

Titles in the World History Series

The Age of Feudalism
Ancient Greece
The Ancient Near East
Architecture
Aztec Civilization
The Crusades
The Cuban Revolution
The Early Middle Ages
Elizabethan England
The End of the Cold War
The French and Indian War
The French Revolution
Greek and Roman Theater
Hitler's Reich
The Hundred Years' War
The Inquisition
The Late Middle Ages
Modern Japan
The Relocation of the North American Indian
The Roman Empire
The Roman Republic
The Russian Revolution
Traditional Japan
The Travels of Marco Polo
Women's Suffrage

WORLD HISTORY SERIES ■■■

Women's Suffrage

by
Miriam Sagan

Lucent Books, P.O. Box 289011, San Diego, CA 92198-9011

PROPERTY OF
KENTLAKE HIGH SCHOOL
LIBRARY MEDIA CENTER
WITHDRAWN

Library of Congress Cataloging-in-Publication Data

Sagan, Miriam, 1954-
      Women's suffrage / by Miriam Sagan.
            p.   cm.—(World history series)
      Includes bibliographical references and index.
      Summary: Chronicles the history of the fight for women's
voting rights, from abolitionism to the feminist movement of
the late 20th century.
      ISBN 1-56006-290-8
      1. Women—Suffrage—United States—History—Juvenile
literature. 2. Feminism—United States—History—Juvenile literature. [1. Women—Suffrage.   2. Women's rights.]
I. Title. II. Series.
JK1898.S34   1995
324.6'23'0973—dc20   95–1276
                                                        CIP
                                                         AC

Copyright 1995 by Lucent Books, Inc., P.O. Box 289011,
San Diego, California, 92198-9011

Printed in the U.S.A.

No part of this book may be reproduced or used in any other
form or by any other means, electrical, mechanical, or otherwise, including, but not limited to photocopy, recording, or
any information storage and retrieval system, without prior
written permission from the publisher.

Contents

Foreword

Each year on the first day of school, nearly every history teacher faces the task of explaining why his or her students should study history. One logical answer to this question is that exploring what happened in our past explains how the things we often take for granted—our customs, ideas, and institutions—came to be. As statesman and historian Winston Churchill put it, "Every nation or group of nations has its own tale to tell. Knowledge of the trials and struggles is necessary to all who would comprehend the problems, perils, challenges, and opportunities which confront us today." Thus, a study of history puts modern ideas and institutions in perspective. For example, though the founders of the United States were talented and creative thinkers, they clearly did not invent the concept of democracy. Instead, they adapted some democratic ideas that had originated in ancient Greece and with which the Romans, the British, and others had experimented. An exploration of these cultures, then, reveals their very real connection to us through institutions that continue to shape our daily lives.

Another reason often given for studying history is the idea that lessons exist in the past from which contemporary societies can benefit and learn. This idea, although controversial, has always been an intriguing one for historians. Those that agree that society can benefit from the past often quote philosopher George Santayana's famous statement, "Those who cannot remember the past are condemned to repeat it." Historians who ascribe to Santayana's philosophy believe that, for example, studying the events that led up to the major world wars or other significant historical events would allow society to chart a different and more favorable course in the future.

Just as difficult as convincing students to realize the importance of studying history is the search for useful and interesting supplementary materials that present historical events in a context that can be easily understood. The volumes in Lucent Books' World History Series attempt to present a broad, balanced, and penetrating view of the march of history. Ancient Egypt's important wars and rulers, for example, are presented against the rich and colorful backdrop of Egyptian religious, social, and cultural developments. The series engages the reader by enhancing historical events with these cultural contexts. For example, in *Ancient Greece*, the text covers the role of women in that society. Slavery is discussed in *The Roman Empire*, as well as how slaves earned their freedom. The numerous and varied aspects of every-day life in these and other societies are explored in each volume of the series. Additionally, the series covers the major political, cultural, and philosophical ideas as the torch of civilization is passed from ancient Mesopotamia and Egypt, through Greece, Rome, Medieval Europe, and other world cultures, to the modern day.

The material in the series is formatted in a thorough, precise, and organized manner. Each volume offers the reader a comprehensive and clearly written overview of an important historical event or period. The topic under discussion is placed in a broad historical context. For example, *The Italian Renaissance* begins with a discussion of the High Middle Ages and the loss of central control that allowed certain Italian cities to develop artistically. The book ends by looking forward to the Reformation and interpreting the societal changes that grew out of the Renaissance. Thus, students are not only involved in an historical era, but also enveloped by the events leading up to that era and the events following it.

One important and unique feature in the World History Series is the primary and secondary source quotations that richly supplement each volume. These quotes are useful in a number of ways. First, they allow students access to sources they would not normally be exposed to because of the difficulty and obscurity of the original source. The quotations range from interesting anecdotes to far-sighted cultural perspectives and are drawn from historical witnesses both past and present. Second, the quotes demonstrate how and where historians themselves derive their information on the past as they strive to reach a consensus on historical events. Lastly, all of the quotes are footnoted, familiarizing students with the citation process and allowing them to verify quotes and/or look up the original source if the quote piques their interest.

Finally, the books in the World History Series provide a detailed launching point for further research. Each book contains a bibliography specifically geared toward student research. A second, annotated bibliography introduces students to all the sources the author consulted when compiling the book. A chronology of important dates gives students an overview, at a glance, of the topic covered. Where applicable, a glossary of terms is included.

In short, the series is designed not only to acquaint readers with the basics of history, but also to make them aware that their lives are a part of an ongoing human saga. Perhaps they will then come to the same realization as famed historian Arnold Toynbee. In his monumental work, *A Study of History,* he wrote about becoming aware of history flowing through him in a mighty current, and of his own life "welling like a wave in the flow of this vast tide."

Important Dates in the History of Women's Suffrage

| 1792 | 1800 | 1810 | 1820 | 1830 | 1840 | 1850 |

1792
Publication of Mary Wollstonecraft's *A Vindication of the Rights of Woman* in England.

1833
William Lloyd Garrison founds the American Anti-Slavery Society.

1837
Angelina Grimké is the first woman to speak in public to a mixed audience of men and women.

1840
Lucretia Mott and Elizabeth Cady Stanton meet.

1843
Oberlin College admits women and African Americans as students.

1845
Lucretia Mott gives the first public suffrage speech in the United States.

1848
Women's Rights Convention is held in Seneca Falls, New York.

1853
Susan B. Anthony begins to work closely with Elizabeth Cady Stanton.

1860
Amendment to the Married Woman's Property Act allows wives to keep their earnings.

1861
Civil War breaks out.

1869
The suffrage movement splits into two factions: the National Woman Suffrage Association led by Elizabeth Cady Stanton and Susan B. Anthony and the American Woman Suffrage Association led by Lucy Stone; the territory of Wyoming allows suffrage for women.

1872
Susan B. Anthony votes illegally in Rochester, New York.

1880
Mary Ann Shadd Cary organizes the Colored Women's Progressive Association which supports suffrage.

| 1860 | 1870 | 1880 | 1890 | 1900 | 1910 | 1920 |

1889
The suffrage associations reunite as the National American Woman Suffrage Association; Wyoming becomes a state, retaining its women's suffrage law.

1894
Colorado passes women's suffrage.

1896
Idaho and Utah pass women's suffrage.

1902
Death of Elizabeth Cady Stanton.

1906
Death of Susan B. Anthony.

1909
Carrie Chapman Catt organizes the Woman Suffrage Party.

1910
Washington passes women's suffrage.

1911
California is won as a women's suffrage state.

1912
Alice Paul founds the Congressional Union for Woman Suffrage, later called the National Woman's Party.

1913
Ida Wells-Barnett and her contingent of African-American women are segregated at a Washington, D.C., suffrage march.

1917
New York passes women's suffrage.

1918
The federal amendment passes the House of Representatives.

1919
The federal amendment passes the Senate.

1920
The Nineteenth Amendment becomes law.

Women and the Ballot

In 1872 Susan B. Anthony, along with her sister and a group of friends, went to register to vote in Rochester, New York. Although at that time it was illegal for women to vote in New York State, by intimidating the registrar they were allowed to register. Using the same methods of intimidation, sixteen women including Anthony, cast their ballots on election day. On Thanksgiving Day, the U.S. chief marshal rang Anthony's doorbell, warrant in hand. He wanted to warn the fifty-two-year-old activist that she would be arraigned (charged) in court for having voted illegally. Anthony refused to answer the summons. Still, the next day, she was taken to the courthouse, along with the other women who had dared to vote. Anthony was charged and released on bail to await trial.

Susan B. Anthony campaigned for equal rights for women, including women's right to vote. Her efforts helped bring about passage of the Nineteenth Amendment, also called the Anthony amendment in her honor.

At the trial Susan B. Anthony admitted that she was indeed guilty of voting. Then the judge allowed Anthony to speak in her own defense, over the objection of the district attorney, who had moved that a woman was not qualified to testify. Although few lawmakers agreed with her position, Anthony reasoned that her right to vote had always existed under the U.S. Constitution. She based this claim in part on the Fourteenth Amendment, which had given the right to vote to African American slaves freed after the Civil War. Anthony claimed that this amendment, written after the Civil War to give former slaves the right to vote, extended to her, a U.S. citizen who was a woman. The judge, who did not agree, levied a hundred-dollar fine. Anthony exclaimed that she would never pay it.

The Women's Suffrage Movement

For Susan B. Anthony and the thousands of American women who campaigned for women's suffrage, the fight did not end in that courtroom. Anthony traveled the country, giving speeches and collecting petitions. In a well-organized political movement, women suffragists managed to convince elected officials and eventually even the president of the United States that women's right to vote should be made law. In 1920 millions of women voted for the first time in a national election. Their right to vote was now protected by the Nineteenth Amendment, which was also called the Anthony amendment, in honor of the woman who had fought long and hard for its passage but

had not lived long enough to cast a legal ballot.

The American women's suffrage movement took more than eighty years to accomplish its goal of gaining women's right to vote, which required the passage of a constitutional amendment. The struggle occurred in two distinct periods. The first, 1840 to 1869, was closely tied to other attempts at reform, such as the abolitionist and temperance movements. It began with an effort to allow women to assume certain rights, such as the right to inherit and own property, and the right to keep their wages.

When the suffrage movement began, society expected middle-class women to conform to a set of prim traditional ideals. These women did not work outside the home, attend college, or express strong opinions in public. They were expected to be good wives and mothers and to see that their households ran smoothly.

Except for a small free minority, African-American women were living their lives in slavery. They had no legal protection of any sort, even the right to raise their own children.

The second period of the suffrage movement, from 1869, when women gained the vote in Wyoming Territory, to 1920, when the Nineteenth Amendment was ratified by Congress, focused more narrowly on the right of women to vote. In part, this was because women had begun to make substantial gains, such as the ability to attend college. African-American women had gained their freedom, if not the right to vote, after the Civil War. By 1920 women from all backgrounds had entered the professions, done work that once only men had done, supported two war efforts, gone west with the frontier,

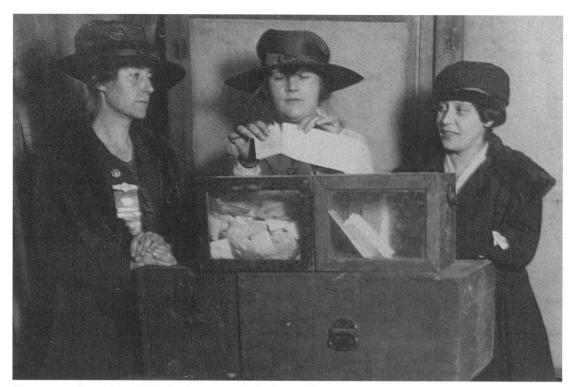

Women exercise their hard-fought right to vote following ratification of the Nineteenth Amendment in 1920.

arrived in cities as immigrants, and achieved more personal and political freedom than their grandmothers could have imagined. Suffrage leaders, heartened by this increase in freedom, believed it was the right time to focus on the vote. During this second period, the women's suffrage movement gained a broad base of support that eventually culminated in the passage of the Nineteenth Amendment.

The road to women's suffrage was long and arduous. As leader Carrie Chapman Catt said, "Women have suffered an agony of soul . . . that you and your daughters might inherit political freedom. That vote has been costly. Prize it!"[1]

Chapter

1 Women and the Abolitionist Movement

In the mid-nineteenth century, women in the United States could not vote in elections, own property, enter into contracts, or attend college. Women were denied these rights and privileges whether they were black or white, free or enslaved, rich or poor. The women's suffrage movement was formed to fight for women's rights as citizens, including the right to vote.

The women who were active in the early suffrage movement were predominantly white and middle class. Many were involved in other reform movements, such as temperance and abolition. The abolitionist movement, in particular, was a training ground for the early suffrage workers.

The abolitionist movement was founded when William Lloyd Garrison formed the American Anti-Slavery Society in 1833. The aim of Garrison's organization was to free the slaves throughout the United States. Garrison was a radical who agitated for the complete and unconditional emancipation of slaves. He also believed in the rights of women. His unusual position, along with the antislavery cause, attracted women to the abolitionist movement.

William Lloyd Garrison was considered a radical because of his support for the emancipation of slaves and for women's rights.

Abolitionist Lucretia Mott

One of these women abolitionists, Lucretia Mott, would go on to lead the women's suffrage movement. Mott was a Quaker, who had grown up on the barren island of Nantucket, Massachusetts, a center of

Lucretia Mott founded her own antislavery organization and later became an influential leader in the women's suffrage movement.

Boarding School. Nine Partners was considered to be an advanced academy that taught serious academic subjects, but the academic level would be equivalent to a high school education today. This was the highest level of education available to women in the United States, and when Lucretia graduated from Nine Partners, she was qualified as a teacher.

The young woman went on to marry another Quaker, James Mott, and she became interested in the abolition of slavery because her religion opposed the institution on moral grounds. She also became a traveling speaker who went from one Quaker meetinghouse to another, an unusual opportunity for a woman. The Quakers were then the only denomination that allowed women to assume leadership roles within the religious community.

Because of her husband's activity as an abolitionist and her own reputation as a liberal abolitionist hostess, Lucretia Mott was invited to observe a meeting of the Anti-Slavery Society. She was one of four Quaker women present. However, Mott and the others were not allowed to actually join the Anti-Slavery Society because most men within the abolitionist movement opposed having women in the organization. As a result, Mott helped to form a group of her own, the Philadelphia Female Anti-Slavery Society. Other women in other northern cities followed suit. Wherever women were excluded from the abolitionist societies, they formed their own separate, if allied, organizations.

Women learned a great deal about political organizing from working in their own groups. By organizing conventions, delivering lectures, and writing petitions, pamphlets, and letters to editors, as well as participating in public debates, women

whaling and fishing. The men of the island were often at sea for months or even years at a time, and the women were quite self-sufficient. Lucretia Coffin Mott's father was a sea captain, and, as a result, her mother led an independent life, running a shop and keeping her own accounts. Mrs. Coffin provided a role model for Lucretia as she took charge of many of the tasks that a man would normally perform. Captain Coffin provided a strong model, as well. The seafarer believed in educating his daughters, and Lucretia was sent to a Quaker academy, the Nine Partners

learned the skills that would be necessary in forming an active women's rights movement.

The most important skill that women developed within the abolitionist movement was the art of public speaking. In the early nineteenth century, women had little opportunity for practice because they were strongly discouraged from public speaking. A woman willing to speak publicly was considered immodest and irreligious at best; at worst she was said to have committed a crime against society and God. These public lectures would become one of the most important tools in the women's suffrage movement. Through lectures, women influenced a change in public opinion that would eventually lead

Woman's Path Laid Open

Margaret Fuller was an early proponent of women's rights, although she died before the suffrage movement had become a force to be reckoned with. Her writing, however, did influence the fight for women's rights. Fuller's book, Women in the Nineteenth Century, *was unlike anything that had ever appeared in the United States. This excerpt is taken from* In Search of Margaret Fuller, *by Abby Slater.*

"We would have every arbitrary barrier thrown down. We would have every path laid open to Woman as fully as to Man. Were this done and a slight temporary fermentation allowed to subside, we should see crystallizations more pure and of more various beauty. We believe the divine energy would pervade nature to a degree unknown in the history of the former ages, and that no discordant collision but a ravishing harmony of the spheres would ensue.

Yet then and only then will mankind be ripe for this, when inward and outward freedom for Woman as much as for Man shall be acknowledged as a *right*, not yielded as a concession. As the friend of the Negro assumes that one man cannot by right hold another in bondage, so should the friend of Woman assume that Man cannot by right lay even well-meant restrictions on Woman. If the Negro be a soul; if the woman be a soul, apparelled in flesh, to one Master [God] only are they accountable. There is but one law for souls, and if there is to be an interpreter of it, he must come not as man or son of man, but as son of God....

What Woman needs is not as a woman to act or rule, but as a nature to grow, as an intellect to discern, as a soul to live freely and unimpeded to unfold such powers as were given her when we left our common home."

to the vote for women. The earliest to speak to a larger crowd were sisters Sarah and Angelina Grimké. They were southern ladies, daughters of a South Carolina slave owner, who came to New York in 1836 to become Quakers and work against slavery. The first woman antislavery workers spoke in private parlors to small groups of other women.

Angelina Grimké: Fiery Orator

Angelina Grimké was a particularly charismatic speaker, able to paint a firsthand ac- count of the evils of life under slavery. Soon her audiences had grown too large for a parlor, and she spoke to groups of women in public auditoriums provided by churches. On an 1837 speaking tour of Massachusetts, men wanted to attend her lectures because of her reputation as a brilliant speaker. When Grimké addressed the mixed crowd, she was condemned by the Massachusetts public and the clergy. A pastoral letter, condemning women who dared to speak in public, was read from pulpits throughout the state.

Sarah Grimké wrote in response: "How monstrous is the doctrine that woman is to be dependent on man! . . . She has surrendered her dearest RIGHTS,

A brilliant speaker, Angelina Grimké (left) braved harsh criticism for daring to speak her views in public. She and her sister Sarah (right) lectured about the evils of slavery to any audience willing to listen.

and been satisfied with the privileges which man has assumed to grant her."[2]

For Sarah Grimké, an attack on a woman who dared to do something men did was not an occasion for an apology but rather a chance to push the cause of women forward. And so, despite the outcry, the Grimkés continued to speak out for abolition to audiences of women and even, when they could find a church sympathetic enough to lend an auditorium, to audiences that included men. The Grimkés' persistence helped lead to more acceptance of women speaking in public.

Mary Wollstonecraft: A Seminal Writer

In addition to abolition, the early suffragists were influenced by a few thinkers and writers who had taken on the issue of women's rights. These included Mary Wollstonecraft, a late eighteenth-century British author, who published *A Vindication of the Rights of Woman*, and Margaret Fuller, American author of *Women in the Nineteenth Century*.

In *A Vindication of the Rights of Woman*, published in England in 1792, Wollstonecraft argued that women and men were equal in their human potential as thinkers and citizens. She emphasized that women must be allowed equal educational opportunities to fulfill their potential. Wollstonecraft's writing became the basis for Lucretia Mott's thinking, and later the women's suffrage movement's position, about the situation of women:

Women are told from their infancy . . . that . . . cunning, softness of temper,

Eighteenth-century author Mary Wollstonecraft wrote A Vindication of the Rights of Woman, *in which she argued that men and women were intellectual equals.*

outward obedience, and that a scrupulous attention to a puerile [childish] kind of propriety [conformity], will obtain for them the protection of men; and should they be beautiful, everything else is needless, for, at least, twenty years of their lives. . . . How grossly do they insult us who thus advise us only to render ourselves gentle, domestic brutes. . . . I may be accused of arrogance; still I must declare that I firmly believe, that all the writers who have written on the subject of female education and manners . . . have contributed to render women more artificial, weak characters, than they would otherwise have been; and consequently, more useless members of society. . . . Many are the causes that, in the present corrupt state of society, contribute to enslave women.[3]

Women and Understanding

Mary Wollstonecraft's A Vindication of the Rights of Woman *was published in England in 1792. Her work inspired the American leaders of the suffrage movement, notably Lucretia Mott and Elizabeth Cady Stanton. In this excerpt from* A Vindication of the Rights of Woman, *Wollstonecraft argues that women need as rigorous an education as do men, otherwise they will be doomed to a second-rate status in society.*

"To do everything in an orderly manner, is a most important precept, which women, who, generally speaking, receive only a disorderly kind of education, seldom attend to with that degree of exactness that men, who from their infancy are broken into method, observe. This negligent kind of guess-work, for what other term can be used to point out the random exertions of a sort of instinctive common sense, never brought to the test of reason, prevents women from learning how to generalize. So women do today what they did yesterday, merely because they did it yesterday.

This contempt of understanding in early life has more baneful consequences than is commonly supposed: for the little knowledge which women of strong minds attain is, from various circumstances, of a more desultory kind than the knowledge of men, and it is acquired more by sheer observations on real life, than from comparing what has been individually observed, with the results of experience generalized by speculation. Led by their dependent situation and domestic employments more into society, what they learn is rather by snatches; and as learning is with them, in general, only a secondary thing, they do not pursue any one branch with that persevering ardour necessary to give vigor to the faculties, and clearness to judgment."

Women of the abolitionist movement, such as Lucretia Mott and the Grimké sisters, saw a link between abolition and the ideas of women such as Wollstonecraft. In fighting for abolition, they hoped not only to abolish slavery but to establish the right to vote for African Americans, men and women alike. By extension, women who were abolitionists assumed that the movement would eventually lead to suffrage for all women. This position was clarified by the Grimké sisters, who wrote about the connection between white women and female black slaves:

> They are our countrywomen—they are our sisters, and to us as women, they have a right to look for sympathy with their sorrows, and effort and prayer for their rescue. . . . Women

ought to feel a peculiar sympathy in the colored man's wrong, for like him, she has been accused of mental inferiority, and denied the privileges of a liberal education.[4]

Elizabeth Cady Stanton: Education as a Firebrand

Another woman who saw the connection between the abolitionist movement and the rights of women had been sensitive to the inequities of women's lives even as a small child. As a youngster, Elizabeth Cady had sat in her father's law office and seen women come to him for advice. For example, a woman who had inherited a farm could not legally protect it if her husband decided to sell it, or had lost it through debt, drunkenness, or gambling. After one such visit, Elizabeth began to cut the laws out of her father's law books with scissors. She mistakenly believed that if she did this, the laws would no longer exist. The attorney explained to his daughter, however, that the laws existed not just in the book but on the records of the state legislature at Albany.

In 1840 Elizabeth Cady married Henry Stanton, an active abolitionist. They set off on their honeymoon to London, to attend the World Anti-Slavery Convention. As

Abolitionists at the World Anti-Slavery Convention in London debated the role of women in their organization. Much to their dismay, the women delegates and speakers were excluded from participating at the convention.

Childhood of a Suffragist

In her autobiography Eighty Years and More, *Elizabeth Cady Stanton, a leader of the American women's suffrage movement, describes her early understanding that girls were not valued as much as boys.*

"The first event engraved on my memory was the birth of a sister when I was four years old. It was a cold morning in January when the brawny Scotch nurse carried me to see the little stranger, whose advent was a matter of interest to me for many weeks after. The large, pleasant room with the white curtains and bright wood fire on the hearth where . . . all kinds of little messes [snacks] which we were allowed to taste were kept warm, was the center of attraction for the older children. I heard so many friends remark, 'What a pity it is she's a girl!' that I felt a kind of compassion for the little baby. True, our family consisted of five girls and only one boy, but I did not understand (until that time) that girls were considered an inferior order of beings."

Later in the book, Stanton speaks of the death of her brother, which confirmed her impression that girls were considered inferior to boys.

"[My father] sat thinking of the wreck of all his hopes in the loss of a dear son, and I wondering what could be said or done to fill the void. . . . At length he heaved a deep sigh and said, 'Oh, my daughter, I wish you were a boy!' Throwing my arms about his neck, I replied: 'I will try to be all my brother was.'

Then and there I resolved that I would not give so much time as heretofore to play, but would study and strive to be at the head of all my classes and thus delight my father's heart."

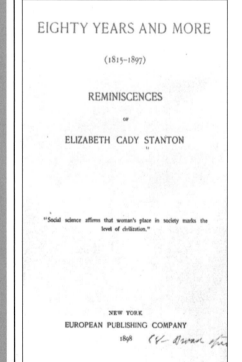

EIGHTY YEARS AND MORE

(1815–1897)

REMINISCENCES

OF

ELIZABETH CADY STANTON

"Social science affirms that woman's place in society marks the level of civilization."

NEW YORK
EUROPEAN PUBLISHING COMPANY
1898

Elizabeth Cady Stanton was a pioneer in the women's suffrage movement. Pictured is the title page from her autobiography Eighty Years and More.

soon as they arrived, the Stantons became embroiled in a conflict over the role of women in the abolitionist movement. The entire first day of business at the convention was taken up not with the cause of abolition but with a debate over whether to recognize the women who were delegates to the convention. The American Anti-Slavery Society, founded by William Lloyd Garrison, wanted to see men and women work together. Garrison believed that women should serve as speakers for the organization and be officers of the society. Women as well as men came to London as delegates and speakers. The National and Foreign Anti-Slavery Society disagreed with Garrison and wanted to exclude women. The two groups battled over the issue of women. Clergymen insisted that the women could not be seated.

Stanton (pictured) joined forces with Lucretia Mott to fight for women's rights following the World Anti-Slavery Convention.

They shook bibles at the men who were willing to seat the women. Throughout the debate, the women were forced to listen in silence. Elizabeth Cady Stanton was profoundly affected by the debates at the World Anti-Slavery Convention and felt humiliated and chagrined. In her autobiography, *Eighty Years and More*, she recounted the scene:

> Though women were members of the National Anti-Slavery Society, accustomed to speak and vote in all its conventions, and to take an equally active part with men in the whole anti-slavery struggle, and were there as delegates from associations of men and women, as well as those distinctively of their own sex, yet all alike were rejected because they were women. Women, according to . . . prejudices at that time, were excluded by Scriptural texts from sharing equal dignity and authority with men in all reform associations; hence it was to [these] minds preeminently unfitting that women should be admitted as equal members to a World's Convention. The question was hotly debated through an entire day. My husband made a very eloquent speech in favor of admitting the women delegates.[5]

But despite the support of such men as Henry Stanton, the women delegates were banned from participation in the convention and allowed to listen only from a special gallery. Elizabeth Cady Stanton pinpointed the moment as the crucial one in awakening her interest in women's rights:

> These feelings [of humiliation] were outweighed by contempt for the shal-

low reasoning of [the women's] opponents and their comical pose and gestures. . . . It was really pitiful to hear narrow-minded bigots, pretending to be teachers and leaders of men, so cruelly remanding [sending back] their own mothers, with the rest of womankind, to absolute subjection to the ordinary masculine type of humanity.[6]

An Important Meeting

One of the delegates banned from the event was Lucretia Mott. Stanton and Mott were staying in the same boardinghouse in London. They soon met and found that they shared a great deal, despite the difference in their ages. Stanton never forgot the impression that Mott made on her. At the time, Lucretia Mott was about fifty-five years old, a modestly dressed woman in traditional Quaker garb: a gray-and-white dress, with starched cap. She was a grandmother who had raised six children of her own. But her gentle appearance belied the strength of her ideas.

Stanton remembered: "As we walked about to see the sights of London, I embraced every opportunity to talk with her. It was intensely gratifying to hear all that, through years of doubt I had dimly thought, so freely discussed by Lucretia Mott and her other abolitionist women."[7]

The meeting with Lucretia Mott was an important event in Elizabeth Cady Stanton's life that would lead to the younger woman's role as a leader of the suffrage movement:

> Mrs. Mott was to me an entire new revelation of womanhood. I sought every opportunity to be at her side, and continually plied her with questions. . . . She told me . . . of Mary Wollstonecraft, her social theories, and her demands for equality for women. I had been reading . . . Mary Wollstonecraft . . . but I had never heard a woman talk about what . . . I had scarcely dared think.[8]

Together, Stanton and Mott resolved to hold a convention as soon as they returned home to launch a society to advocate the rights of women. Although they did not follow their plan until eight years later, the groundwork was laid that would lead directly to the Women's Rights Convention in Seneca Falls.

Thus, frustration experienced in the abolitionist movement led to the birth of the suffrage movement. The abolitionist movement was the crucible that turned middle-class women into savvy political organizers who were able to sway audiences to their point of view.

Chapter

2 The Convention for Women's Rights at Seneca Falls

For the eight years following their first meeting in London, Elizabeth Cady Stanton and Lucretia Mott were not idle in their fight for women's rights. Mott continued to think, write, and speak on the subject. In 1845 she gave the first speech by a woman to a public audience in the United States on the topic of women's suffrage. She further refined her thinking on the subject when she wrote her "Discourse":

> We deny that the present position of woman is her true sphere of usefulness; nor will she attain to this sphere, until the disabilities and disadvantages, religious, civil, and social, which impede her progress, are removed out of her way. These restrictions have enervated [weakened] her mind and paralyzed her powers. While man assumes that the present is the original state designed for woman, that the existing differences are not arbitrary . . . but grounded in nature, she will not make the necessary effort to obtain her just rights, lest it should subject her to the kind of scorn and contemptuous manner in which she has been spoken of.[9]

Elizabeth Cady Stanton was somewhat hindered in her political work by domestic and family life, and the demands of rais-

Stanton first lobbied for the right of married women to own property.

ing young children. The family settled in Boston, which was a hub of intellectual and radical activity. Here Stanton met the notable abolitionists of the day, as well as women who were independent thinkers. The atmosphere of Boston helped Stanton further develop her own philosophies and in a milieu of antislavery meetings, lectures on every subject, and debates, she observed the forums that would soon be

Many of the skills and philosophies that Stanton brought to the women's rights movement she learned while attending antislavery meetings and debates.

part of the tools of the movement to secure the rights of women.

Married Women and Property

Stanton also became involved in her first political battle for women's rights. While Lucretia Mott had received most of her political training in the abolitionist movement, Stanton's first fight was to allow a married woman to own property. At the time, the laws of most states ruled that all property, money, and wages acquired by a woman before or after marriage were owned by her husband.

By 1836, a bill to protect the property of married women was introduced into the New York state legislature. The original organizers of the bill were Ernestine Rose, a Polish-Jewish immigrant, and Pauline Wright, an upper-class young woman from the western part of the state. In 1840 Stanton joined them in the fight

to pass the bill. In her first exposure to the techniques of lobbying, she gained skills that would serve her well in the suffrage movement. She went door to door to collect signatures on a petition in support of the bill, gave public speeches, and spoke to committees at the legislature. In April 1848 the bill finally passed in New York State. It was not a complete victory, however. Married women, while allowed to control their own inheritance and property, still did not own their wages, which were the property of their husbands. This was a particular hardship to working-class and farming women, who were seamstresses, domestics, and hired laborers on farms owned by someone else's family. Middle-class women, who were unlikely to work after marriage but did often have substantial inherited property, benefited greatly from the passage of the act. Still, the bill was an improvement in women's status. And, most important, it gave women—in particular, Elizabeth Cady Stanton—the sense that they could fight and win certain rights.

Life in Seneca Falls

During her years in Boston, Stanton was in the midst of activity. In 1847, however, Henry Stanton decided to move his family to Seneca Falls, in the Finger Lakes region of central New York, where he could practice law with his father-in-law. The move was not a happy one for his wife, who felt isolated in the small town. She was discontent and felt trapped in her domestic role.

In Seneca Falls, my life was comparatively solitary, and the change from Boston was somewhat depressing. There, all my immediate friends were reformers. . . . Here our residence was on the outskirts of the town, roads very often muddy and no sidewalks most of the way, Mr. Stanton was

---

Education of Girls

In the nineteenth century, a debate raged over whether women should be admitted to institutions of higher education. Sarah Sewell, an antisuffragist writer, took the view "Against Higher Education for Women," excerpted from Strong Minded Women and Other Lost Voices from 19th Century England, *by Janet Murray.*

"The education of girls need not be of the same extended, classical, and commercial character as that of boys; they want more an education of the heart and feelings, and especially of firm, fixed, moral principles. They should be made conversant with history, geography, figures, the poets, and general literature, with a sure groundwork of religion and obedience. [But they should not be educated further because] a profoundly educated woman rarely makes a good wife or mother. The pride of knowledge does not mix well with their every-day matter of fact rearing of children, and women who have stored their minds with Latin and Greek seldom have much knowledge of pies and puddings, nor do they enjoy the hard and uninteresting work of attending to the wants of little children; and those women, poor things, who have lost their most attractive charm of womanliness, and are seen on the public platforms, usurping the exclusive duties of men, are seldom seen in their nurseries; though they may become notorious themselves, their children rarely do them credit, and the energy they throw away upon the equalizing bubble, would be much better expended in a more womanly and motherly manner, in looking after their husbands' comforts, the training of their children, and the good of the household at large."

---

frequently away from home, I had poor [unsatisfactory] servants, and an increasing number of children. To keep a house and grounds in good order, purchase every article for daily use, keep the wardrobes of a half dozen human beings in proper trim, take the children to dentists, shoemakers, and different schools, or find teachers at home, altogether made sufficient work to keep one brain busy, as well as all the hands I could impress into service. Then, too, the novelty of housekeeping had passed away, and much that was once attractive in domestic life was now irksome.[10]

The situation Stanton describes was the common one of any housewife in the nineteenth, or even twentieth, century. For Stanton, however, it was an impetus to action:

My experience at the World's Anti-Slavery Convention, all I had read of the legal status of women, and the oppression I saw everywhere, together swept across my soul, intensified now by many personal experiences. It seemed as if all the elements had conspired to impel me to some onward step. I could not see what to do or where to begin—my only thought was a public meeting for protest and discussion.[11]

Stanton had a chance to renew her revolutionary vigor when she and Lucretia Mott met again on July 13, 1848. Mott was in the Finger Lakes area, and mutual friends had invited Stanton to visit for the day. Stanton remembered:

There I met several members of different families of Friends [Quakers],

Mott asked her husband James to chair the Seneca Falls convention because she feared that a woman-led convention would be considered too radical.

earnest, thoughtful women. I poured out, that day, the torrent of my long-accumulating discontent, with such vehemence and indignation that I stirred myself, as well as the rest of the party, to do and dare anything. My discontent . . . must have been healthy, for it moved us all to prompt action.[12]

The Women's Rights Convention

Stanton and Mott immediately began to plan a public meeting to discuss the rights of women and to protest their condition. They announced to the public that a Women's Rights Convention would meet the following week at the Wesleyan Chapel

A Fashionable School

In the 1830s, in both England and the United States, young women could not attend college. Instead, middle-class young ladies were often sent to fashionable boarding schools, where they might learn French or music, but little beyond a superficial level. Frances Power Cobbe described her experiences at such a boarding school in "A Fashionable Finishing School," quoted in Strong Minded Women and Other Lost Voices from 19th Century England, *by Janet Murray.*

"The din of our large double schoolrooms was something frightening. Sitting in either of them, four pianos might be heard going at once in rooms above and around us, while at numerous tables scattered about the rooms there were girls reading aloud to the governesses and reciting lessons in English, French, German, and Italian. This hideous clatter continued the entire day till we went to bed at night, there being no time whatever allowed for recreation, unless the dreary hour of walking with our teachers (when we recited our verbs) could be so described by a fantastic imagination. In the midst of this uproar we were obliged to write our exercises, to compose our themes, and to commit to memory whole pages of prose. . . .

On the whole, looking back after the long interval, it seems to me that the young creatures there assembled were full of capabilities for widely extended usefulness and influence. . . . But all this fine human material was deplorably wasted. Nobody dreamed that any one of us could in later life be more or less than an 'Ornament of Society.' . . . Everything was taught us in the inverse ratio of its true importance. At the bottom of the scales were Morals and Religion, and at the top were Music and Dancing, miserably poor music, too."

Colleges were closed to women in the early nineteenth century. Instead, many women were sent to fashionable boarding schools where their education was limited to such subjects as music, dancing, and religious instruction.

at Seneca Falls. A week was an extremely short time even for seasoned political organizers to plan a convention. Stanton admitted that these were hasty steps but also noted that the speed of putting the convention together did not allow her to hesitate in fear.

The Women's Rights Convention was held on July 19 and 20. The first day was for women only, and the second day was open to anyone who wanted to participate. But despite the radical nature of the enterprise, even Stanton and Mott did not dare to have the convention led by a woman. This would have been unthinkable at a time when even the separate women's antislavery societies were headed by men. James Mott, Lucretia's husband and a strong advocate of women's rights, agreed to chair the convention.

The convention had been publicly announced in the *Seneca County Courier.* It attracted about three hundred people, forty of whom were men. The women who attended were an unusual mixture of radical friends of Stanton's and local women and girls from upstate New York farming families. While Quaker and abolitionist women might be assumed to be in favor of women's rights, the attendance of local farmers encouraged Stanton and Mott to think that women's rights might attract a broader audience.

Typical of the farming women who attended was seventeen-year-old Charlotte Woodward, who lived four miles from Seneca Falls. A teacher in a local school, she was not able to keep any of her wages, which were claimed by her father. Excited by the prospect of women's rights, Woodward borrowed the farm cart and set off for the convention. Charlotte Woodward would be the only woman to live to see the goals of the convention realized. In 1920, at the age of ninety, Woodward cast her first ballot.

The Women's Rights Convention discussed many issues, including women's suffrage. Stanton wanted to focus the convention by drawing up a Declaration of Sentiments and Resolutions, which would then be discussed and voted upon. Although such a vote had no legal power, Stanton hoped it was a way to create a public agenda for the convention and to make sure that certain points were discussed. A ratification of resolutions also would allow the press to be informed of what positions the conference supported.

We Hold These Truths to Be Self-Evident

Stanton took the Declaration of Independence as a model for the Seneca Falls Declaration of Sentiments and Resolutions. She used the language of this famous document to assert the rights of women. Stanton's declaration began, "We hold these truths to be self-evident: that all men and women are created equal; that they are endowed by their Creator with certain inalienable rights." It continued, "The history of mankind is a history of repeated injuries and usurpations on the part of man toward woman, having in direct object the establishment of an absolute tyranny over her."[13]

Stanton then outlined the basic ways in which women had been oppressed by men: women had been denied the vote, denied higher education, denied economic opportunity, and excluded from religious leadership. The Declaration of

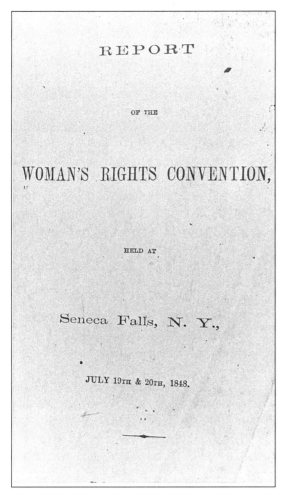

The title page from the report of the Seneca Falls Women's Rights Convention.

had the effect of preventing women from speaking in public. Of all the resolutions, however, the one that asked for the vote for women was the most radical. "It is the duty of the women of this country to secure to themselves their sacred right to the elective franchise."[14]

For Stanton, the convention became a launching point for leadership. Not only had she written the declaration, but she read it in public, a much more frightening task. A woman who spoke in public in 1848 had to conquer not only stage fright but also the deeply felt social prohibitions against a woman taking any sort of public role. For Stanton, though, the speech she gave on the first day of the convention marked the start of a career in which she would speak on women's rights on hundreds of occasions across the country.

The second day of the convention was devoted to voting on the Declaration of Sentiments and Resolutions. All the points were accepted, except for the article calling for women's suffrage. A debate raged over whether the convention should actually call for the vote for women. Many of the participants felt the demand was just too radical. They were afraid of a major public outcry that would make the new women's rights movement look ridiculous, crushing it before it had started. Even radical Lucretia Mott felt that the demand for the vote might be too extreme. She worried that it would detract from other, seemingly appropriate demands and alienate possible supporters. Henry Stanton, Elizabeth Cady Stanton's usually supportive husband, was also shocked by the demand for suffrage. Only Frederick Douglass, a well-known abolitionist who was a former slave, supported the proposal for women's suffrage in his newspaper, *The North Star.*

Sentiments and Resolutions was a radical document and a call to women to fight for their rights. With the exception of the right to vote, which was finally won in the twentieth century, Stanton's concerns have remained the issues of the women's movement in the United States until the present.

The specific resolutions at the end of the document attacked laws that discriminated against women, a double standard of morality, and the social customs that

Famous abolitionist Frederick Douglass spoke at the Seneca Falls convention in support of women's suffrage.

Douglass spoke at the convention, as well, insisting that the vote was an absolute necessity for women. Without the vote, women would ultimately have no protection of their rights and no way to influence lawmakers.

The resolution for women's suffrage passed by a small margin. If the demand for suffrage could shock a convention dedicated to women's rights, then its effect on society at large would surely be even greater.

A Public Outcry

The convention had been a small event in an obscure location. However, ripples from news of the declaration were felt almost immediately. Stanton herself was surprised to see newspapers across the country respond.

> No words could express our astonishment on finding, a few days afterward, that what seemed to us so timely, so rational, and so sacred, should be a subject for sarcasm and ridicule to the entire press of the nation. With our Declaration of Rights and Resolutions for a text, it seemed as if every man who could wield a pen prepared a homily [little sermon] on "woman's sphere" [woman's proper place in society]. All the journals, from Maine to Texas, seemed to strive with each other to see which could make our movement appear the most ridiculous. The anti-slavery papers stood by us . . . but so pronounced was the popular voice against us, in the parlor, press, and pulpit, that most of the ladies who had attended the convention and signed the declaration, one by one, withdrew their names and influences.[15]

Local newspapers had first reported on the convention, and because its content was novel if not downright shocking, the large New York papers soon picked up the story. Most of their editors were appalled by the resolutions at Seneca Falls. One man wrote: "This bolt is the most shocking and unnatural incident ever recorded in the history of humanity [and it will] degrade from their high sphere and noble destiny women of all respectable and noble classes, and prove a monstrous injury to all mankind."[16]

The majority of newspapers in the country denounced the event. Editors in print and pastors from the pulpit attacked the convention and the women who had sponsored it, calling them everything from unfeminine Amazon warriors to spinsters who lacked love and family. Cartoons depicted the women of Seneca Falls as ugly, masculine, even cigar-smoking creatures. One of the few major news organs to support the convention was the *New York Tribune*, published by Horace Greeley, in New York City.

Stanton and Mott had not expected so much media attention nor the almost complete focus on women's suffrage. However, despite the negative coverage, the call for women's rights took hold and grew. Just a few weeks after the Seneca Falls convention, a group of Quaker women held another conference in Rochester. With Mott and Stanton in attendance, this body also voted in support of the women's suffrage resolution. In 1850 four such women's rights conventions were held in Ohio. The same year, a National Woman's Rights Convention was held in Massachusetts. These conventions, inspired by the one at Seneca Falls, served as meeting places for women interested in suffrage and other issues important to women. They served as the start of an organized base for the movement.

The Seneca Falls convention, the platform on which Elizabeth Cady Stanton emerged as a leader, was the start of the fight for women's rights in the United States. The issues outlined at the convention would remain the important ones for the women's rights movement, including

The New York Tribune, *published by Horace Greeley (above), was one of the few news organizations that supported the Women's Rights Convention. Most coverage of the event was negative, such as this editorial cartoon that pokes fun at the convention's feminist participants.*

Eyewitnesses at Seneca Falls

Mehitable Haskell attended the Women's Rights Convention in Seneca Falls, New York. In 1851 she described her reaction, quoted in The Ladies of Seneca Falls, *by Miriam Gurko.*

"This meeting, as I understand it, was called to discuss Woman's Rights. Well, I do not pretend to know exactly what woman's rights are; but I do know that I have groaned for forty years, yea, for fifty years, under a sense of woman's wrongs. I know that even when a girl, I groaned under the idea that I could not receive as much instruction as my brothers could. I wanted to be what I felt I was capable of becoming, but opportunity was denied me. . . . I rejoice that so many women are here; it denotes that they are waking up to some sense of their situation."

Charlotte Woodward, who attended the convention as a teenager, wrote with similar feeling. This excerpt, too, is from The Ladies of Seneca Falls.

"Most women accepted . . . society as normal and God-ordained, and therefore changeless. But I do not believe that there was any community anywhere in which the souls of some women were not beating their wings in rebellion. . . . Every fiber of my being rebelled, although silently, all the hours I sat and sewed gloves for a miserable pittance [very low wages] which, after it was earned, could never be mine [because Woodward was obliged by law to turn the money over to her father]. I wanted to work, but I wanted to choose my task and I wanted to collect my wages."

the most radical demand for women's suffrage. However, at this point in the movement, all the demands were considered to be of equal importance, including the right to be educated and to speak in public. In addition, Seneca Falls and the conventions that followed would act as magnets for other women interested in suffrage. Notably, the high-visibility convention at Seneca Falls led two important future leaders, Susan B. Anthony and Lucy Stone, to join the movement.

Chapter

3 Susan B. Anthony and the Women's Movement of the 1850s

During the 1850s, the decade before the outbreak of the Civil War, the fledgling women's movement began to organize itself. The movement's leaders honed their agenda to focus on full rights and participation in civic life for women. Leaders such as Elizabeth Cady Stanton grew to be skilled speakers and organizers of petitions as well during this period.

Women's rights had achieved a high level of visibility after the convention at Seneca Falls. Soon, many other women were drawn to the movement, but none would be more important than Susan B. Anthony, whose name would eventually become synonymous with the fight for women's suffrage in the United States.

Susan B. Anthony shared a similar background with Lucretia Mott and Elizabeth Cady Stanton. Like Mott, Anthony had been raised in a Quaker family that emphasized equality for women. Like Mott and Stanton, she had a father who believed in education for girls as well as boys. Susan B. Anthony also attended a Quaker boarding school in Philadelphia, where she studied science and other subjects sometimes considered too advanced for girls. Anthony then went to work as a teacher, one of the few professions open to women. But instead of working toward abolition, Anthony became a member of

another major reform movement of the day—the temperance movement, an organized effort to end the abuse of alcohol. Just as Mott and Stanton had learned many skills of political organizing in the abolitionist movement, Anthony learned these through the temperance movement. Also like Mott and Stanton, she was excluded from public leadership on the basis of her sex.

Susan B. Anthony was raised in a family that stressed education and equality for women.

A temperance procession in Philadelphia. The temperance movement blamed alcohol for many of the ills plaguing society and worked to make alcohol illegal.

Anthony was younger than Mott and Stanton, and her political experience was formed by the most recent reform of the time, the temperance movement. Many women blamed the ills of society, and women's lot in general, on the effects of alcohol. Alcohol led to wife-beating, domestic violence, and poverty for the wives of drinkers these reformers argued. For these reasons, the temperance movement had many women as members and would eventually have women as leaders. At first, however, the movement did not specifically support rights for women.

Anthony joined the Daughters of Temperance, became an officer in the organization, and soon made her first speech in public. She eventually became the president of the Rochester chapter of the Daughters of Temperance and learned how to organize conventions and raise money to support the cause. However, Anthony was not allowed to speak at the New York State temperance convention. The male chairman barred her, saying, "The sisters were not invited here to speak, but to listen."[17] In what might have been a rerun of the World Anti-Slavery Convention, Anthony and her followers walked out and formed a separate organization, the Woman's State Temperance Society. Men were allowed to join this society, and men held all the leadership positions.

Anthony was not only frustrated with male dominance of the Temperance Society but by what she perceived as women's general powerlessness in society. Women were hampered, she realized, both by not having their own money and by not being able to vote to change laws.

By 1853 Susan B. Anthony's frustration would lead her to concentrate her energies on women's rights rather than temperance. She attended the third National Woman's Rights Convention, held in Syracuse, New York, and soon thereafter began to work closely with Elizabeth Cady Stanton. Stanton knew immediately that she and Anthony would function well as a leadership team. Stanton, in the years of

Miss Anthony

In her autobiography Eighty Years and More, *Elizabeth Cady Stanton remembered her first impression of Susan B. Anthony, who was to become her closest collaborator and friend.*

"Owing to early experience of the disabilities of her sex, the first demand for equal rights for women found echo in Susan's heart. And, though she was in the beginning startled to hear that women had actually met in convention, and by speeches and resolutions had declared themselves man's peer in political rights, and had urged radical changes in State constitutions and the whole system of American jurisprudence; yet the most casual review convinced her that these claims were but the logical outgrowth of the fundamental theories of our republic.

At this stage of her development, I met my future friend and co-adjutor [fellow worker] for the first time. How well I remember the day! [Abolition leaders] George Thompson and William Lloyd Garrison having announced an anti-slavery meeting in Seneca Falls, Miss Anthony came to attend it. These gentlemen were my guests. Walking home, after the adjournment, [Stanton and her husband] met Mrs. Bloomer and Miss Anthony on the corner of the street, waiting to greet us. There she stood, with her good, earnest face and genial smile, dressed in gray delaine [a material], hat and all the same color, relieved with pale blue ribbons, and perfection of neatness and sobriety. I liked her thoroughly, and why I did not invite her home with me to dinner, I do not know. She accuses me of neglect, and has never forgiven me, as she wished to see and hear all she could of our noble friends. I suppose my mind was full of what I had heard, or my coming dinner, or the probable behavior of three mischievous boys who had been busily exploring the premises while I was at the meeting."

Anthony and Stanton in their later years. With strengths that complemented each other, the two women formed an effective and efficient team.

were one, and in the division of labor we exactly complemented each other. In writing we did better work than either could alone. While she is slow and analytical in composition, I am rapid and synthetic. I am the better writer, she the better critic. She supplied the facts and statistics, I the philosophy and rhetoric, and, together, we have made arguments that have stood unshaken through the storms of long years; arguments that no one has answered. Our speeches may be considered the united product of our two brains.[18]

At the time she met Anthony, Stanton was the mother of seven children and thoroughly tied to the concerns of housekeeping and motherhood. For many years, she was unable to travel freely to do organizing and public speaking for the women's suffrage movement. Anthony, in contrast, was a single woman, free to devote herself full-time to the cause. Stanton summed up their style of teamwork when she said of Anthony, "I forged the thunderbolts and she fired them."[19]

A Working Team

One of the first issues Stanton and Anthony worked on as a team was the issue of property rights for married women. The Married Woman's Property Act had been passed in New York State in 1848. However, there were still gross inequities for married women under the law. A married woman could not sell her property or own the wages she had earned. The lack of legal status for married women was an ongoing issue for the early women's rights

their association, would be more of the intellectual and writer, while Anthony would be more of a hands-on leader and speaker. Stanton recalled:

Thus, whenever I saw that stately Quaker girl coming across my lawn, I knew that some happy convocation of the sons of Adam was to be set by the ears, by one of our appeals or resolutions. The little portmanteau [valise], stuffed with facts, was opened. . . . Then we would get out our pens and write articles for papers, or a petition to the legislature. . . . We never met without issuing a pronunciamento on some question. In thought and sympathy we movement. If women could not enter into contracts, it was unlikely that they could ever win such a right as suffrage.

And so the first major struggle for women's rights after the Seneca Falls convention was petitioning for married women's property rights. The fight against unfair treatment under the law became a rallying point for Stanton and Anthony. Anthony called a convention of women to discuss the matter. On a fund-raising trip for the convention, Anthony wrote:

> Thus as I passed from town to town was I made to feel the great evil of woman's utter dependence on man. I never before took in so fully the grand idea of pecuniary independence. Woman must have a purse of her own [which can be obtained] only through legislation. If this is so, then the sooner the demand is made, the sooner it will be granted. It must be done by petition, and this, too, of the very next legislature.[20]

At a women's rights convention in Rochester, Anthony recruited sixty women to cover the sixty counties of New York State. Armed with petitions, Anthony and the others went door to door, asking for signatures. The petitions asked the New York legislature to pass a law giving married women the same rights as men to write a will, keep their earnings, and have guardianship over their children. In ten weeks, Anthony and her supporters had collected sixty thousand signatures. On the strength of the petition, the legislature allowed Elizabeth Cady Stanton to give a speech for the bill.

Stanton, tied to her large and demanding household, did not collect signatures. For Anthony and the sixty women who went door to door, the collection of signatures was political work of a consciousness-raising sort. Many women slammed doors in their faces, saying they were content to let their husbands make the decisions and did not need legal rights. Yet many other women were persuaded to support the movement through this same campaign. In thousands of conversations, grassroots support of women's rights began to be evident all over New York State—twenty times as many people signed the petition as had attended the first women's rights convention six years earlier. Anthony was an invaluable leader of the burgeoning movement in that she not only worked hard but was capable of mobilizing large groups of volunteers, who in turn stimulated support on the grassroots level.

Putting Pressure on the New York Legislature

Stanton, by contrast, had her strength as a speaker. In 1854 she spoke before the legislators in Albany, describing the plight of married women. A wife, Stanton reminded her listeners, "has no civil existence, no social freedom. . . . She can own nothing, sell nothing. She has no right even to the wages she earns; her person, her time, her services are the property of another. . . . She can get no redress for wrongs in her own name."[21]

Despite Stanton's effort, the issue met with ridicule, even within the legislature itself. In 1855 the report of a committee of the New York legislature on women's rights took a facetious and ironic tone when it reported:

An illustration depicts Stanton demonstrating her greatest strength–her public speaking ability–at a women's rights convention.

The bachelors on the committee, with becoming diffidence [reserve], have left the subject pretty much to the married gentlemen. They have considered it with the aid of the light they have before them and the experience married life has given them. Thus aided, they are enabled to state that the ladies always have the best place and choicest tidbit at the table. They always have the best seat in the cars, carriages, and sleighs; the warmest place in winter and the coolest place in summer. They have their choice on which side of the bed they will lie, front or back. A lady's dress cost three times as much as that of a gentleman; and, at the present time, with the prevailing fashion, one lady occupies three times as much space in the world as a gentleman.[22]

This humorous and unsympathetic response was typical of the antisuffrage position of the day. Eventually, the legislature was won over on more serious grounds, although it was not until March 1860 that the New York state legislature passed an amendment to the Married Woman's Property Act, allowing wives to keep their earnings. Stanton and Anthony had not expected their pressure on the legislature to lead to immediate results. Instead, they kept up year after year, with Anthony traveling to lecture and hold meetings, petitioning, and setting up local women's rights organizations. Stanton continued to give her well-researched speeches before the legislature. The amending of the Married Woman's Property Act was indeed a victory, but perhaps equally important, in achieving that victory, Stanton and Anthony had built a political base from which they could continue to operate.

Wearing Bloomers

One other issue that was important to Stanton and Anthony in the early years of their collaboration was the seemingly more frivolous one of "dress reform," or "bloomerism." Stanton and Anthony, like other middle-class women of their time, were expected to wear long skirts made of

Stanton favored bloomers (below) over the more restrictive corsets and long dresses that women were expected to wear at the time (right). However, public outrage forced her to stop wearing the comfortable and practical outfit.

five yards of fabric. Beneath these voluminous skirts were hoops and petticoats. Tightly bound corsets of whalebone were also worn in order to give a woman a "fashionable" if unnatural hourglass shape. In these restrictive outfits, it was difficult for a woman to move freely, and almost impossible for her to exercise. Whalebone corsets made it difficult to breathe, and women often fainted while wearing them. Long skirts that dragged in muddy, garbage-filled streets were not only a nuisance but a health hazard.

Amelia Bloomer, who had introduced Elizabeth Cady Stanton to Susan B. Anthony, was a Quaker, active in the temperance movement. She had attended the first women's rights convention at Seneca Falls and became a convert to the feminist cause. As a clothing reformer, Bloomer popularized the outfit that came to bear

Females in Trousers

"Bloomers" were the first dress reform for American women. They made an impression on all who saw them, including British writer Jane Ellen Panton, who reminisced about them in "A Memory of Bloomers," reprinted in Janet Murray's book.

"[I saw] two females, in long trousers tied at the ankles, and with a short species of stuck-out skirt similar to the one a ballet dancer used to wear. They had hats and feathers and soft grey boots with shiny leather toes, and were altogether awesome specimens of humanity. They were turning round the corner at the edge of our crescent, and we were told that the females were called 'Bloomers,' so it must have been the year of the great exhibition, when the original Mrs. Bloomer first came over from America to teach her doctrine of hygienic clothing. . . . [T]hese Bloomers were followed by the ubiquitous [ever-present] street boy making use of all possible derogatory [insulting] terms. At the same time . . . these erratic [unusual] females were the first persons who ever made women aware of the fact that they possessed legs, and that they should use them more than they did in those days. . . . When I recollect the walks I used to take, holding yards of material in my cramped hand, while petticoats twisted and twined themselves around my unfortunate limbs, and that I used to skate in a similar garb, the long skirt being then drawn by pulleys into folds so that it did not entirely impede one's progress, I envy the girls of to-day."

"BLOOMERISM," OR THE NEW FEMALE COSTUME OF 1851,

As it has appeared in the various Cities and Towns.

BOSTON: S. W. WHEELER, 66 Cornhill—1851.

Women who dared to wear bloomers were ridiculed and criticized by a public who largely considered the new outfit too radical.

her name—soft, loose-fitting, ankle-length trousers, worn under a long loose tunic.

For Stanton, freedom in dress represented freedom of choice in all things for women. The bloomer outfit was practical, and Stanton enjoyed it particularly as a maternity dress and when she was busy caring for her children. She wrote:

> This dress makes it easier to do all these things—running from cradle to writing desk, from kitchen to drawing room, singing lullabies at one moment in the nursery and . . . ditties the next moment on the piano stool. If I had long skirts, how could I accomplish this?[23]

The public outcry against bloomers, however, rivaled the outrage directed at women speaking in public or even demanding the vote. Men and boys verbally attacked women wearing the outfit and threw eggs and stones at them in the street. The press printed doggerel, cartoons, and editorials against the outfit. After several years of ridicule, even Elizabeth Cady Stanton and Amelia Bloomer herself stopped wearing bloomers. However, by about 1880 the outfit had made a comeback, particularly when bicycles became a sports rage for both sexes. The bloomer was also, in its own way, the great-grandmother of contemporary dress reform, in which pants and other comfortable work clothes are as acceptable for women as for men.

Antisuffrage Backlash

With the advent of a formal women's rights movement in the 1850s, there was also a backlash against all aspects of women's rights, particularly from ministers and newspaper editors. In 1852 the *New York Herald* characterized the workers for women's rights in unflattering, hostile terms:

> Some of them are old maids, whose personal charms were never very attractive, and who have been sadly slighted by the masculine gender in

Former slave and well-known abolitionist Sojourner Truth. She is remembered most for a fiery and impassioned speech she delivered at a women's rights convention in 1851.

general; some of them women who have badly mated; some, having so much of the virago [loud, bossy woman] in their disposition, that nature appears to have made a mistake in their gender—mannish women, like hens that crow . . . there is [also] a class of wild enthusiasts and visionaries— very sincere, but very mad [crazy]. . . .

Of the male sex who attend these conventions for the purpose of taking part in them, the majority are hen-pecked husbands, and all of them out to wear petticoats.[24]

Certain suffrage leaders spoke directly to those who said that women should stay content in their usual role. Among the most famous responses was a speech made at a women's rights convention in Akron, Ohio, in 1851 by Sojourner Truth, a former slave. Hostile ministers had continually interrupted the speakers, when Sojourner Truth rose and addressed the assembly:

That man over there says that women need to be helped into carriages, and lifted over ditches. . . . Nobody ever helps me into carriages or over mud-puddles. . . . And aren't I a woman? Look at me! Look at my arm! I have ploughed, and planted, and gathered into barns [a biblical phrase that would have been familiar to Truth's hearers], and no man could head me! And aren't I a woman? I have borne thirteen children, and seen 'em most all sold off into slavery, and when I cried out with a mother's grief none but Jesus heard me! And aren't I a woman?[25]

This stirring speech remains a well-known call for women's rights over a hundred years later. At the time, however, neither women in slavery nor those who were free could vote.

Nevertheless, the women's movement and the fruitful partnership between Elizabeth Cady Stanton and Susan B. Anthony sustained these attacks and continued to gain momentum. Stanton and Anthony concentrated the early years of the U.S. suffrage movement on reform, whether the legal reform of the laws affecting women and property or the dress reform of comfortable bloomers. With each issue, they built interest in their cause, either with grassroots organization or with media coverage. However, more than half a century of intensive political organizing would be necessary for a majority of men and women to change their minds about woman's proper place. Stanton, Anthony, and other leaders still needed to develop a larger political base from which to launch the ideals of women's suffrage.

Chapter

4 The Civil War and the Passage of the Civil Rights Amendments

During the 1860s, the women's suffrage movement had to struggle to keep the issue of women's rights alive in the public eye. This was because the nation was in the midst of upheaval of a different sort—the Civil War and its painful aftermath.

When the Civil War broke out between the North and South in 1861, the majority of women on both sides threw themselves into the war effort. Women immediately went to work as nurses. In the North, they were supervised by Dorothea Dix, who had brought the profession into respectability, in part by hiring only women who were over thirty and considered plain looking. With men off at war, women ran farms, plantations, and businesses. They also worked as clerks in offices, as teachers, and in factories. But although women found themselves suddenly propelled out of a so-called proper woman's sphere and into a larger world of work, this change would not have any positive impact on the rights of women until the war was over.

For Elizabeth Cady Stanton and Susan B. Anthony, the abolition of slavery and a victory for the North temporarily became a first priority. The last women's rights convention on the Seneca Falls model was held in New York in February 1861. Two months later, the nation was at war, and neither Stanton, Anthony, nor anyone else

As superintendent of U.S. Army nurses during the Civil War, Dorothea Dix helped to bring respectability to the nursing profession.

had the time or energy for organizing conventions on women's suffrage. Instead, Stanton and Anthony threw their considerable leadership ability, as well as the talents of their constituents, into forming the Women's National Loyal League,

Lincoln on Slavery

In the nineteenth century, the institution of slavery, like the second-class status of women, was sometimes considered to be divinely decreed. Abraham Lincoln attacked this thinking with his speech "On Pro-Slavery Theology," collected in Lincoln: Speeches, Letters, Miscellaneous Writings.

"Certainly there is no contending against the Will of God; but still there is some difficulty in ascertaining and applying it, to particular cases. For instance we will suppose the Rev. Dr. Ross has a slave, and the question is 'Is it the Will of God that this slave shall remain a slave, or be set free?' The Almighty gives no audible answer to the question, and his revelation—the Bible—gives none. . . . No one thinks of asking the slave's opinion on it. So, at last, it comes to this, that Dr. Ross is to decide the question. And while he considers it, he sits in the shade, with gloves on his hands, and subsists on the bread that the slave is earning in the burning sun. If he decides that God wills the slave to continue a slave, he thereby retains his own comfortable position; but if he decides that God wills the slave to be free, he has thereby to walk out of the shade, throw off his gloves, and delve for his own bread.

But, slavery is good for some people!!! As a good thing, slavery is strikingly peculiar, in this, that it is the only good thing which no man ever seeks the good of, for himself.

Nonsense! Wolves devouring lambs, not because it is good for their own greedy maws, but because it is good for the lambs!!!"

Abraham Lincoln challenged the argument that the Bible contained proof that slavery was the will of God.

which circulated a petition demanding freedom for slaves. In the spring of 1861, they collected four hundred thousand signatures to support the abolitionist and Republican Party cause. At the time, Stanton and Anthony both believed that if slaves were free and granted the right to vote, women would most probably be included in the constitutional amendments that would be necessary to guarantee those rights. The Women's National Loyal League petition helped to generate extensive support of the Thirteenth Amendment to the U.S. Constitution, which abolished slavery. Stanton and Anthony had long supported the abolitionist cause and they also expected positive results for the status of women.

Freedom for the Slaves but No Votes for Women

When the Civil War ended, however, it was clear that the power of the federal constitution was required to establish and protect the rights of former slaves. The Emancipation Proclamation of January 1, 1863, had freed the slaves in states that had seceded from the Union, and in thirty-two words the Thirteenth Amendment, ratified in 1865, had put an end to the institution of slavery. The Fourteenth Amendment, which covers several broad areas of citizenship and civil rights, as well as issues not touching directly on the lives of former slaves, was not ratified until 1868.

During the period of debate over the provisions of the Fourteenth Amendment, various drafts were circulated throughout the country, and public-spirited citizens made it a point to study them. It was

known, for example, that the proposed amendment would make all former slaves U.S. citizens, with all the attributes of citizenship, including the right to vote. It was also understood that the amendment would impose penalties on any state that disenfranchised a citizen over the age of twenty-one and barred that person from voting. Women leaders, who had assumed that this provision implied that it would be illegal to deny suffrage for women, as well, were shocked to learn that the Fourteenth Amendment voted on by Congress excluded their gender. Section 2 of the amendment contains the words: "But when the right to vote . . . is denied to any male inhabitant of such state . . ."[26]

Blacks cast their ballots following passage of the Fifteenth Amendment, which granted black males the right to vote but excluded women.

A Question of Life and Death

Frederick Douglass had long been a supporter of abolition and women's suffrage. Yet he supported the passage of the Fifteenth Amendment, which would give the right to vote to newly freed black men. In these excerpts from a speech recorded in The History of Woman Suffrage, *Douglass emphasizes the greater necessity of the vote for black men.*

"I must say that I do not see how anyone can pretend that there is the same urgency in giving the ballot to woman as to the Negro. With us, the matter is a question of life and death. . . . When women, because they are women, are hunted down through the cities of New York and New Orleans, when they are dragged from their houses and hung upon lamp posts; when their children are torn from their arms, and their brains dashed upon the pavement; when they are objects of insult and outrage at every turn; when they are in danger of having their homes burnt down over their heads; when their children are not allowed to enter schools; then they will have an urgency to obtain the ballot equal to our own. . . .

Yes, yes, yes [this is also] true for the Black woman but not because she is a woman but because she is Black!"

The word "male" appears only once in the U.S. Constitution: in the Fourteenth Amendment. Throughout, senators and members of the House of Representatives are designated as "Persons" or "Citizens," and there is no language barring women from serving as ambassadors, judges, or military commanders. The president is always referred to as "he," but it is now taken for granted that this wording does not mean that a woman, if elected to that office, could not serve.

Plainly, though, the Fourteenth Amendment disenfranchised not only African-American women who were newly freed slaves but the women of both races who had worked for abolition and now believed that suffrage for all was in sight. Anthony, Stanton, and the other women who had supported first the abolitionist cause and then, in the Civil War, the side of the Union, felt deeply betrayed. Stanton wrote:

The only way [our senators and representatives] could open the constitutional door just wide enough to let the Black man pass in was to introduce the word "male" into the Constitution. After the generous devotion of . . . women . . . in sustaining the policy of the Republicans, both in peace and war, they felt it would come with a bad grace from that party to place new barriers in woman's path to freedom. But the amendment was [not] written without the word "Male."[27]

The Republican Party, which held national power after the war, was indeed indebted to the women who had supported it to victory. However, Republican leader Charles Sumner, abolitionist Wendell Phillips, and newspaper editor Horace Greeley were not prepared to repay that debt. In part, they felt that enfranchising black males was all the change the country could bear. They felt that women's suffrage was considerably less important and would have to wait. Horace Greeley, who normally supported women's suffrage, personally and in the *Tribune* refused to help Stanton and Anthony:

> This is a critical period for the Republican party and the life of the Nation. . . . It would be wise and magnanimous [noble] in you [women] to hold your claims . . . in abeyance until the Negro is safe . . . and your turn will come next. I conjure [beg] you to remember that this is "the Negro's hour" and your first duty now is to go through the State and plead his claims. . . . [I]f you persevere . . . you need depend on no further help from me or the *Tribune*.[28]

Stanton and Anthony responded immediately to the wording of the Fourteenth Amendment. As Stanton recalled, "We at once sounded the alarm, and sent out petitions for a constitutional amendment to prohibit the States from disenfranchising any of their citizens on the ground of sex. [We] made haste to rouse . . . women . . . to the fact that the time had come to begin vigorous work again for woman's enfranchisement."[29] However, women's suffrage leaders were unable to change the wording of the amendment. The Fifteenth Amendment specifically permitted men of any race, regardless of whether they had ever been slaves, to vote, but it did not enfranchise women of any race.

A Divisive Issue

Not all the usual supporters of women's suffrage agreed with the stance taken by Susan B. Anthony and Elizabeth Cady Stanton. In May 1869, four years after the end of the Civil War, Stanton and Anthony formally renewed the women's rights movement by convening a meeting of a new organization, the Equal Rights Association. However, the Fifteenth Amendment was still a divisive issue. Frederick Douglass wanted the meeting to endorse the Fifteenth Amendment, pleading that it was only right that the vote be given to black men first. Stanton and Anthony felt betrayed when the majority of the members of the Equal Rights Association agreed with Douglass and supported the Fifteenth Amendment, despite its exclusion of women.

Sojourner Truth did not support the Fifteenth Amendment. She was afraid that if African-American women were not given the vote, they would suffer what Elizabeth Cady Stanton had called "a triple bondage that man never knows."[30] Sojourner Truth commented pointedly:

> There is a great stir about colored men getting their rights, but not a word about the colored women, . . . and if colored men get their rights, and not colored women theirs, you see the colored men will be masters over the women, and it will be just as bad as

African-American women sawmill workers in the early twentieth century. Despite their strong support for women's rights, black women were largely excluded from the white suffrage movement.

it was before. . . . For Black women go out washing, which is about as high as a colored woman gets, and their men go about idle, strutting up and down; and when the women come home they ask for their money and take it all, and then scold because there is no food.[31]

However, not all African-American women agreed with Sojourner Truth. Some felt that suffrage for African-American men was a first step for all newly freed slaves. This attitude did begin to change, though, in the decades of struggle for women's suffrage that followed the Civil War. By the end of the nineteenth century, African-American women were unusual in that as a group they supported the issue of women's suffrage completely. In part, this was for sound economic reasons. Out of necessity, more African-American

women worked outside the home than did their white counterparts. The black churches also supported women's suffrage. And the majority of black men, including such prominent spokesmen as Frederick Douglass and reformer W. E. B. Du Bois, also supported women's suffrage. As Du Bois realized, "Votes for women means votes for Black women," and therefore more political clout for the African-American community as a whole.[32]

African-American Women and Women's Rights

Between 1865 and 1920, however—that is, from the end of the Civil War until the ratification of the Nineteenth Amendment—African-American women were basically excluded from the white suffrage movement. Repeating the experience of the women who had been excluded from the abolitionist and temperance movements, African Americans had to form their own institutions to work for suffrage. This was in large part due to the general atmosphere of segregation and racial discrimination that permeated the United States after the Civil War. Although the former slaves were free, they were far from equal. All over the country, schools, churches, and neighborhoods were segregated by race. The segregation of African-American women within the suffrage movement was part of the social norm, which in this case was extremely racist and discriminatory.

In the same way that the women abolitionists had formed their own groups, African-American women formed social and political clubs after the Civil War and throughout the Reconstruction period in the South. These clubs allowed black women to come together and work on shared concerns. In 1880 Mary Ann Shadd Cary organized the Colored Women's Progressive Association, whose goals included suffrage.

Like all the advocates of women's rights, African-American women believed they could have a positive effect in the United States. However, they continued to face the double oppression of race and sex discrimination. Suffragist Josephine St. Pierre Ruffin wrote:

> All over America, there is to be found a large and growing class of earnest, intelligent, progressive colored women, who, if not leading full useful lives, are only waiting for the opportunity to do so, many of them warped and cramped for lack of opportunity, not only to do more, but to be more; and yet, if an estimate of the colored women of America is called for, the inevitable reply, glibly given is, "For the most part ignorant and immoral, some exceptions of course, but those don't count."[33]

And as suffragist Adella Hunt Logan noted, if "white women needed the vote to acquire advantages and protection of their

A freedmen's school is burned by whites in the South. While blacks were freed from the bonds of slavery following the Civil War, they still faced widespread racial discrimination and segregation.

"Are We to Be Left Out?"

African-American women faced discrimination even in black organizations after the Civil War. In 1869 the National Colored Labor Union held its founding meeting. A woman delegate expressed disappointment at the way concerns of working women were being neglected in these remarks, quoted in When and Where I Enter, *by Paula Giddings.*

"[I] was much disappointed that in all your deliberations, speeches and resolutions, which were excellent so far as the men are concerned, the poor women's interests were not mentioned, or referred to . . . are we to be left out? We who have suffered all the evils of which you justly complain? Are our daughters to be denied the privilege of honestly earning a livelihood by being excluded from the milliner [hatmaker], dressmaker, tailor, or dry good [department] store, in fact every calling that an intelligent, respectable, industrious female may strive to obtain, and this merely because her skin is dusky? These privileges are all denied colored females of Newport. However well they may be fitted for other positions, they are compelled to accept the meanest drudgeries or starve. . . .

Therefore the colored women of Newport would ask your meeting and Convention that is to assemble next Monday to remember us in your deliberations so that when you mount the chariot of equality, in industrial and mechanical pursuits, we may at least be permitted to cling to the wheels."

rights, then Black women needed the vote even more so."[34]

That the women's suffrage movement as a whole, however, did not welcome the support of African-American women seems tragically hypocritical. They justified this in several ways. In part, Stanton and Anthony felt they had been betrayed by black leaders who had supported the amendments that granted former slaves the vote but not women. More insidiously, white women saw the exclusion of blacks as a way to get more male support for their cause in the southern states. Throughout the South, white suprema-

cists wanted to continue to keep African-American men from voting.

White supremacists after the Civil War began to see that enfranchising women might help their segregationist cause. They reasoned that white women as voters might help keep African Americans in an economically and politically inferior position. Stanton herself was not above playing on these fears when she lobbied for women's suffrage:

In view of the fact that the Freedom of the South and the millions of foreigners now crowding our shores, most of whom represent neither property, education, nor civilization, are all in the progress of events to be enfranchised, the best interests of the nation demand that we outweigh this incoming pauperism [poverty], ignorance and degradation, with the wealth, education, and refinement of the women of the republic.[35]

By the turn of the century, there were local and statewide black suffrage clubs all over the country to help organize the fight for women's suffrage. Their members collected tens of thousands of signatures on petitions, passed resolutions, and gave speeches. Lottie Rollins was the first African-American woman to give a speech to the South Carolina Women's Rights Association. Rollins was from a family that had been free in prewar Charleston, and like other women suffrage leaders, came from a supportive and liberal background. She addressed the meeting with these words:

> It had been so universally the custom to treat the idea of woman suffrage with ridicule and merriment that it becomes necessary in submitting the subject for earnest deliberation that we assure the gentlemen present that our claim is made honestly and seriously. We ask suffrage not as a favor, nor as a privilege, but as a right based on the ground that we are human beings and as such, entitled to all human rights.[36]

Although on a personal level, Susan B. Anthony was a liberal who did not and would not tolerate racism in her home, when African-American women asked her to help them organize a branch of the National Woman Suffrage Association, she refused. She felt it would reflect negatively

Black journalist Ida Wells-Barnett was angered by the discrimination she encountered in the national suffrage associations.

on the organization. Ida Wells-Barnett, who was an African-American journalist and newspaper owner, as well as a personal friend of Anthony's, argued strongly against this attitude. The two women had long discussions, but often disagreed. Wells-Barnett often pointed up the evils of racism to her friend, but Susan B. Anthony believed that all social ills would be healed when women got the ballot. Wells-Barnett accused Anthony of believing that a utopian millennium would come with women's suffrage—this was the polite equivalent of saying that someone believes in the tooth fairy—and Anthony admitted that that was exactly right. Anthony was also afraid of alienating the white southern women in her organization, most of whom were segregationists who would not have tolerated the presence of African-

American women. At no time did the national suffrage associations take a stand against segregation, even when their own delegates were victims of discrimination in trains or restaurants. As late as 1913, Ida Wells-Barnett was told by white women suffrage leaders that her contingent had to walk in the rear of a huge suffrage march. Essentially, the leaders of the women's suffrage movement found it inexpedient to include a fight against racism on their agenda, much as the abolitionists had chosen not to fight for women's rights.

A Split in the Movement

In 1869 the mainstream suffrage movement split into two factions over the issue of the Fifteenth Amendment. Anthony and Stanton, who opposed the amendment, met and organized the National Woman Suffrage Association, with Stanton as president. In response, Lucy Stone, a leader of the moderates who had supported the Fifteenth Amendment, formed the American Woman Suffrage Association. The two suffrage factions would not reunite until 1890.

Along with Mott, Stanton, and Anthony, Lucy Stone was one of the four major leaders of the women's suffrage movement in the nineteenth century. Of the four, Stone had the most formal education. She attended Oberlin College, which opened in Ohio in 1833. By 1843, Oberlin had become the first college in the United States to admit both women and African Americans. It was the only college in the country to award degrees to women.

At Oberlin, Lucy Stone wrote a brilliant essay that was to be used during the

Lucy Stone founded the more moderate faction of the suffrage movement, the American Woman Suffrage Association. Unlike the National faction, it included men among its ranks.

graduation ceremony. Forbidden to read the essay in public because she was a woman, Lucy Stone refused to allow the piece to be read at all, even by a professor. And so at college, Stone not only received an unusually good education for a young woman, she also experienced being silenced simply because of her sex.

Although of a younger generation than Mott and Stanton, Lucy Stone began her career as a political organizer in the abolitionist movement. Like Susan B. Anthony, she also believed in temperance. By 1850 Stone was busy lecturing full-time on the subjects of temperance, abolition, and women's rights. She spoke extensively in public on behalf of the Massachusetts Anti-Slavery Society. And she helped to or-

Oberlin College, which in 1843 became the first college in the United States to admit both women and blacks.

ganize a women's rights convention in Massachusetts.

As an orator, Lucy Stone had a lovely speaking voice that was often described as silvery or bell-like. Of all the leaders of the women's suffrage movement, she was the most natural speaker. Even as a paid abolitionist speaker, Stone could not help inserting demands for women's rights into her antislavery speeches. She believed in self-determination for women: "Too much has already been said and written about woman's sphere. . . . Leave women, then, to find their sphere. And do not tell us before we are born even, that our province is to cook dinners, darn stockings, and sew on buttons."[37]

Lucy Stone was active in the women's rights movement throughout the Civil War. By the time the split came to the move-ment, she had the experience and political clout to lead the more moderate faction, the American Woman Suffrage Association. Stone felt that the methods used by Anthony and Stanton were too radical. For example, Stone believed that women needed an alliance with men to further their aims. Her organization included men, and she remained loyal to the party of the abolitionists—the Republicans—even though women had been excluded from the electoral process by the Fifteenth Amendment. In contrast, the National faction, headed by Stanton and Anthony, had no men as members and no party affiliation.

The split between Stone's organization and the one headed by Anthony and Stanton would lead to two different approaches toward the passage of an amendment to ensure women's suffrage.

5 The Changing Role of Women

The period between 1869 and 1890 was a time of expansion for the role of America's women. Women became much more visible in public life, even though they had not yet attained the right to participate in elections. The area that was considered to be "woman's sphere" was changing. For middle-class women, much of this was due to increased education. Now able to attend colleges as well as secondary-level boarding schools, middle-class women often spent a few years on their own, away from the demands of family, before they settled into marriage.

For the increasing number of college-educated women, however, the professions opened slowly. Women were accepted as teachers, and after the Civil War as nurses. Both these careers could be seen as an extension of the nurturing role that was expected of women. Yet the majority of college-educated women still chose marriage and family as an avocation. In order to receive intellectual stimulation, these women began to form clubs. Women's clubs were serious endeavors that encouraged intellectual pursuits, organized reading groups, and sponsored

A nurse-training program in 1890. By the late nineteenth century women were slowly entering professions like nursing and teaching.

Frontier women endured the same hardships and were often expected to do the same work as their male counterparts. The result was a greater respect for women which furthered the cause of women's suffrage in the West.

cultural events. The women attracted to the club movement were often less radical than those who worked for suffrage. However, these groups across the country gave women a forum to meet and discuss issues. They raised money for charity and influenced their communities. The clubs brought middle-class women out into the public sphere. And eventually their members did support the suffrage cause.

Middle-class African-American women had their own club movement, which unanimously supported women's suffrage. The majority of African-American women were still struggling to survive economically after emancipation from slavery. Although for the most part in the South they continued to work long hours farming and doing field work, they attained some economic independence when their families moved to cities and they continued to work outside the home. After the Civil War, African-American women acquired as much education as possible, and they still worked hard to support their children's ability to go to school.

The area of American society that was most open to change for women was the frontier. As the boundaries of the country expanded toward the Pacific Ocean, women went along with men as settlers. Far from the social constraints of nineteenth-century East Coast society, women often did the so-called men's work: plowing, farming, carrying guns. Women endured hardships along with men, earning a kind of respect for their strength and endurance that no lady in a parlor ever received. It was no coincidence that the western states were the first to grant suffrage to women—it was the natural outgrowth of an egalitarian frontier society.

The younger generation of women in every walk of American society grew up with more concrete expectations that women should have rights. These changes affected the tactics of the women's suffrage movement and also brought it closer to its goal.

The Suffrage Movement Expands

The period between 1869 and 1890 was a tumultuous one for the women's suffrage movement. The two rival suffrage organizations, the National Woman Suffrage Association, and the American Woman Suffrage Association, continued to clash and define themselves separately.

Although the groups both fought for suffrage, they maintained different approaches. The National Woman Suffrage Association focused on trying to pass a federal suffrage amendment. The American Woman Suffrage Association worked for suffrage on the local and state levels. Eventually, a combination of the approaches of both associations would be needed to win the vote for women.

As a rule, the women who supported Stone's American association were more moderate. They were often from the East, and cities such as Boston, which had a reputation for decorum. The constituency of Stanton and Anthony's National association included younger women and pioneer women from the expanding western frontier. To the westerners, the names of Stanton and Anthony were synonymous with women's rights. They supported the National association, which they felt would try to gain the vote through any means necessary.

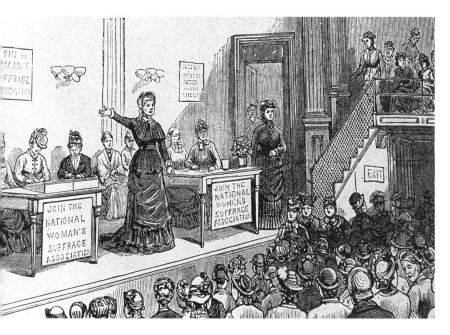

Led by Stanton and Anthony, the National Woman Suffrage Association focused their energies on the creation and passage of a federal suffrage amendment. Younger women and pioneer women were especially attracted to the organization.

Pioneer Memories

Pioneer women's lives were hard. In "Memories of a Handcart Pioneer, with Some Account of Frontier Life in Utah and Nevada," settler Mary Ann Hafen recollected the hard tasks she had faced. This quotation is excerpted from Christiane Fischer's Let Them Speak for Themselves: Women in the American West, 1849–1900.

"On May 6, 1891, with me and our five children tucked into a covered wagon, John clucked at the horses and drove away from our old home town. . . . As neighbors, relatives and friends crowded about to see us off, I with others shed a few tears. . . . I knew . . . that my children were to grow up in a strange land with scarcely a relative near; and that they too would have to share in the hardships of subduing a new country. . . .

The big lot [in the new home] already had five or six almond trees growing, and a nice vineyard of grapes. But there was a little wash running through the side of the lot which had to be filled in; and there was only a makeshift fence of mesquite brush piled about three feet high. Besides, the lot was covered with rocks, because it was close to the gravel hill. . . .

As soon as we could we planted corn, cane, squashes and melons in the field. . . . The brush fences were but poor protection from the stray animals that went foraging about. However we got a pretty good crop from everything planted that year. [We] dug up three young mulberry trees from Mesquite and planted them around our shadeless home. Now, after forty-seven years of growth, those mulberry trees completely shade the old place."

The life of a pioneer woman was hard. Survival meant working long hours at many strenuous tasks.

The role of the western states in the fight for women's suffrage was crucial. It was on the western frontier, with its notions of equality and rights for women, that the first serious gains for women's suffrage were made. In 1869 the territory of Wyoming became the first government in the United States to give women the

unreserved right to vote. This was an ab-
solutely crucial victory for the forces of
suffrage—its first major success, which
would serve as a model for many other
western states.

Wyoming Grants Women the Vote

The passage of women's suffrage in
Wyoming directly resulted from a speech
Susan B. Anthony gave in Peru, Illinois.
Her lecture on the cause of women's suffrage impressed Esther Morris, a six-foot-
tall woman in the audience, who was
about to move to Wyoming. Morris took
the message of suffrage with her.

*A champion of women's suffrage in Wyoming,
Esther Morris later became the first woman justice of
the peace in the United States.*

Gold had been discovered in
Wyoming, and there was now a small set-
tlement, South Pass City, which was a clas-
sic Wild West town, full of saloons and
sharpshooters. Esther Morris saw economic opportunity there and went into
business. At the time, Wyoming was a
rowdy, uncivilized place, but in 1869 it was
formally established as a territory of the
United States. Esther Morris tried to woo
the new government leaders into support-
ing suffrage by entertaining important legislators at her home, always repeating
Anthony's arguments to them. Esther
Morris would go down in history as "the
mother of suffrage in Wyoming." This
fighter for women's rights would also become the first woman justice of the peace
in the United States.

One of Morris's guests went on to introduce a bill in the Wyoming legislature
that gave women the vote, as well as pro-
viding equal pay for men and women and
explicitly acknowledging women's right to
own property.

This radical package of laws support-
ing women's rights had no precedent in
any state or territory of the United States,
and few legislators expected it to become
law. It was passed, in part, because at the
time Wyoming's two-party system was in a
state of confusion. The Democrats, who
had proposed the women's suffrage law,
were at first trying to embarrass the Republican governor, who they felt sure
would veto such a suffrage bill. Republicans in the house of representatives of the
territory did vote for the bill, as their party
prided itself on radicalism and support of
women's rights. Some of the men who
voted for the law, however, did so under
the assumption that the measure would be
vetoed. Much to the surprise of almost

A Hard Day's Work

In the West, women worked at whatever jobs came to hand. Mary Mathews described this flexibility in "Ten Years in Nevada, or Life on the Pacific Coast." The excerpt is taken from Let Them Speak for Themselves.

"I was still washing, teaching, and sewing.

Perhaps the reader would like to know how I managed to do it.

I got up early every Monday morning, and got my clothes all washed and boiled and in the rinsing water; and then commenced my school at nine. At noon I spent my leisure time sewing; and after school I did the same after I got my supper out of the way. I often sewed till twelve and one o'clock at night. After all was quiet, I could do a great deal of sewing.

Tuesday morning I had my clothes on the line by daylight, and my breakfast ready.

After breakfast my work was soon done up, and I sewed again until nine o'clock.

At noon I starched all my clothes. After school I ironed as many of them as I could, and at night finished the rest of them. Then I had the rest of the week to sew in; but I could not lay up money very fast. . . .

[In the boardinghouse] I had twenty-six beds to make up and rooms to take care of, and all the washing and ironing to do. Well, I can tell you, it was pretty hard. I got up early. While many of my neighbors were sleeping, I was doing up the work of those roomers who had gone to work on the six o'clock shift. If it was Monday, I would pick up all of the dirty clothes together, then I would come down and get my breakfast, do up the dishes, and then sit down and make four or five ticks [mattresses] before dinner-time. . . .

There were repairs constantly to be made, but I managed to keep up with the whole of it by working every night till twelve and one o'clock."

everyone, the governor decided the bill was reasonable and signed it into law. He was affected by the fact that twenty years earlier he had attended one of the early women's rights conventions in Ohio and had been so swayed by the speakers that he became a supporter of women's suffrage.

Women at the polls in Wyoming, which in 1889 became the first state to pass a women's suffrage bill.

After the bill was passed, opponents predicted that there would be fighting at the polls between pro- and antisuffrage factions. But all went smoothly. Both the Democratic and Republican parties set out to woo women voters, and the polls were closely watched to keep out any men who might harass the new voters. Although women's suffrage began in Wyoming as the result of a confused partisan fight, when Wyoming became a state in 1889, it retained its laws for women's rights and suffrage. The passage of the women's suffrage bill in Wyoming was an important first step for the suffrage movement across the country.

The Western Frontier

Susan B. Anthony and Elizabeth Cady Stanton soon made the western frontier their focus. As the suffrage movement gained momentum in the West, Anthony and Stanton crisscrossed the country, giving speeches on women's suffrage.

By now, Stanton's children were grown, and she had the freedom to travel. Conditions were often difficult, and travel by train and carriage over harsh terrain was exhausting. But Stanton was seemingly indefatigable. Even in the worst circumstances, she persevered in order to spread the word of her cause:

> We reached [the railroad station] at three o'clock in the morning. As the depot . . . was nearly half a mile on the other side of the town, I said to a solitary old man who stood shivering there to receive us, "How can I get to the other station?"
>
> "Walk, madam."
> "But I do not know the way."
> "There is no one to go with you."
> "How is my trunk going?" said I.
> "I have a donkey and cart to take that."
> "Then," said I, "you, the donkey, the trunk, and I will go together."
>
> So I stepped into the cart, sat down on the trunk, and the old man laughed heartily as we jogged along through the mud of that solitary town in the pale morning starlight. Just as the day was dawning, [the town] with

Mothers in Wagons

In the campaign for women's suffrage in the western states, Elizabeth Cady Stanton remembered the struggle of pioneer women. This passage is from Stanton's book Eighty Years and More.

"In toasting 'the women of Nebraska,' at the meeting, I said, 'Here's to the mothers who came hither by long, tedious journeys, closely packed with restless children in emigrant wagons, cooking the meals by day, and nursing the babies by night, while the men slept. Leaving comfortable homes in the East, they endured all the hardships of pioneer life, suffered, with the men . . . prairie fires, and the devastating locusts. Man's trials, his fears, his losses, all fell on woman with double force; yet history is silent concerning the part woman performed in the frontier life of the early settlers. Men make no mention of her heroism and divine patience; they take no thought of the mental or physical agonies women endure in the perils of maternity, ofttimes without nurse or physician in the supreme hour of their need, going, as every mother does, to the very gates of death in giving life. . . .

Traveling all over these western states in the early days, seeing the privations women suffered, and listening to the tales of sorrow at the fireside, I wondered that men could ever forget the debt of gratitude they owed to their mothers, or fail to commemorate their part in the growth of a great people. Yet the men of Nebraska have twice defeated the woman suffrage amendment."

its rough hills and bold scenery, loomed up. Soon, under the roof of . . . one of the distinguished lawyers of the West, with a good breakfast and sound nap, my night's sorrows were forgotten.[38]

In 1871 Anthony and Stanton went as far as California, holding suffrage meetings in the major cities along the way, from New York to San Francisco. From 1869 to 1873, they toured Iowa, Missouri, Illinois, and Nebraska. Anthony often gave speeches to the general public on women's suffrage, while Stanton presented separate afternoon lectures to women only on the more "delicate" subjects of "Marriage and Maternity." Stanton remembered: "We spoke in jails, prisons, asylums, depots, and the open air. Wherever there were ears to hear, we lifted up our voices, and, on the wings of the wind, the glad tidings were carried to remote corners."[39]

East Coast Cities

It was a labor-intensive task for Stanton and Anthony, perhaps more difficult for Anthony, who was not a natural public speaker and had to push herself to perform. But it was an effective tactic, resulting first in the influence on Esther Morris, which led to the passage of women's suffrage in Wyoming, and later to the move for other states to follow suit and give women the right to vote.

One other frontier besides the expanding West was open to women after the Civil War. The large East Coast cities were flooded with immigrants from eastern Europe. Many women immigrants worked in the garment industry or as domestic workers. And women, both immigrant and native born, began to work in industry and factories. African-American women emigrating from the South to northern cities swelled the ranks of working women. White-collar work also opened to women. Before the Civil War, only men had operated typewriters, but by 1900 a third of all clerical workers were women.

In factories and offices, women's hourly wages were about half what men earned. Facing economic discrimination on the job, women often joined the newly organized unions to strike for higher wages. Susan B. Anthony supported the emerging labor movement as it fought for higher wages, shorter hours, and safer conditions for both men and women. She formed the Workingwoman's Association to help organize working women in various industries. Although the women's suf-

Women rapidly joined the ranks of the working class in industries and factories on the East Coast. However, they were regularly hired at half the salary of men.

frage movement would remain essentially a concern of middle-class women, the labor unions gave a whole new segment of American women the opportunity to fight for their rights. Eventually, the labor unions would give organized support to the Nineteenth Amendment and aid in its passage.

Suffrage Movement Reunited

In 1890 suffrage groups all over the United States, including Lucy Stone's American group, were reunited under the banner of the National American Woman Suffrage Association. Elizabeth Cady Stanton served as president for the next two years. She resigned in 1892 at the age of seventy-seven. Susan B. Anthony became the next president of the organization—she was seventy-two at the time. The original leadership of the women's suffrage movement was aging. Lucretia Mott had died in 1880. And none of the original four leaders of the movement—Mott, Stanton, Anthony, and Stone—would live to see the passage of a federal amendment guaranteeing the right to vote to women.

When the women's movement was reunited in 1890, it was a strong political organization, with grassroots groups all over the nation and strong support on the west-

Labor unions were formed to help working women organize for higher wages, shorter hours, and improved working conditions.

ern frontier. The movement was no longer the dream of a few visionary reformers. In 1893, in a bold speech at the Chicago World's Columbian Exposition, an African-American woman named Frances Harper said: "Today we stand on the threshold of woman's era. In her hand are possibilities whose use or abuse must tell upon the political life of the nation, and send their influence for good or evil across the tract of unborn ages."[40]

The next thirty years of the struggle for women's suffrage would prove her words true.

6 Changes at the Turn of the Century

The turn of the century saw the emergence of the "New Woman," who earned her own living, and the end of the traditional ideal of woman as perfect wife and mother, happily confined to the parlor. During the 1890s American life was changing for both men and women. Increasingly, people moved to the hubs of large cities and away from smaller communities. By 1890, 19 percent of women in the United States were working outside the home. Of these, only 14 percent were married, but by 1920 that figure had grown to 23 percent. The ideal of female beauty had changed, too, away from women wearing corsets and heavy skirts. Now a popular illustration of the Gibson Girl—an athletic-looking young woman in a free and easy dress—represented the fashion aspirations of many.

By 1900 the United States boasted five thousand women who had graduated from college, something their mothers and certainly their grandmothers had

Fashion reflected the changing roles of women. The athletic and freer fashion ideal of the 1920s reflected the greater independence achieved by women.

The powerful Women's Christian Temperance Union (WCTU) lobbied for an amendment prohibiting the manufacture and sale of alcohol. WCTU members were also strong supporters of women's suffrage.

scarcely dared to dream of. Negro colleges that had been built in the South after the Civil War admitted women as well as men in a push for economic and social self-sufficiency for the descendants of slaves. African-American women from middle-class backgrounds entered the teaching profession, although they usually taught at segregated institutions. As a result of these changes, it was increasingly difficult for educated women, and women who worked outside the home, whether in the professions or in factories, to docilely accept their inability to vote.

Between about 1890, when the suffrage groups reunited, and about 1906, when Susan B. Anthony died, the movement for women's suffrage in the United States entered a new phase. At this time, suffrage was becoming respectable, and it

was no longer a social outrage for women to speak in public. On two fronts, the role of women was changing and expanding. On the western frontier, women had more control over their lives and in some respects were equal to men. In the workforce, women were entering both the professions and industrial work. Women had more economic clout, and they were also gaining political influence in the states and territories where they could vote. Trade unions supported women's suffrage, as did a powerful temperance organization, the Women's Christian Temperance Union (WCTU). All these positive factors put the women's suffrage movement on the cusp of success. Supporters of women's suffrage had gone from being a tiny minority to approaching a majority of men and women in the United States.

Suffrage in the States

It was in this context of change that the fight for women's suffrage was first won on the level of the states. Between 1869 and 1917, sixteen states granted women the vote. The fight for suffrage in the states and territories was difficult and required some new leadership. The struggle was not only a legal one but a political and philosophical one against the last vestiges of antisuffrage feeling in the United States.

Antisuffrage

The original opponents of women's suffrage had often taken the view that it was God's will for men to dominate women. Some of the nineteenth-century opponents of suffrage declared that the granting of women's rights would break up the family. Others explained that women did not need the right of suffrage because women were on a pedestal—they were so good and pure that they were nobler than men and needed to be protected by them instead of given rights under the law. The antisuffrage attitudes reflected the prevailing attitudes of the time expressed by Charles Dickens in his novel Oliver Twist: "The prerogative of man is to command . . . the prerogative of woman is to obey."[41] Editorials in newspapers sounded a similar note: "Everyone knows that men and women are not equal in all things. I do not believe that good women *want* the ballot; but even if they did, the question which man must determine is not affected by what women *want*, but by what they *ought* to have."[42]

It was not only men who opposed women's suffrage. Women also organized

Passersby stop to read literature posted at the headquarters of the National Association Opposed to Woman Suffrage, an organization of women who feared that women's suffrage would lead to strained relations between husbands and wives.

A Woman's Voice

Elizabeth Cady Stanton died in 1902. She had wanted not only the vote for women but the liberation of women as individuals. Her ideas would be echoed in the feminist movement more than half a century later. This expression of her philosophy is excerpted from Elizabeth Griffith's In Her Own Right: The Life of Elizabeth Cady Stanton.

"No matter how much women prefer to lean, to be protected and supported, nor how much men prefer to have them do so, they must make the voyage of life alone, and for safety in an emergency they must know something of the laws of navigation. . . . The talk of sheltering women from the fierce storms of life is sheerest mockery, for they beat on her from every point of the compass, just as they do on man, and with more fatal results, for he has been trained to protect himself, to resist, to conquer. . . . Whatever the theories may be of woman's dependence on man, in the supreme moments of her life he cannot bear her burdens. . . . The strongest reason why we ask for woman a voice in the government under which she lives; in the religion she is asked to believe; equality in social life, where she is the chief factor; a place in the trades and professions, where she may earn her bread, is because of her birthright to self-sovereignty; because, as an individual, she must rely on herself."

to fight it. Organizations such as the Boston Committee of Remonstrants [vigorous objectors] and the Association Opposed to Woman Suffrage were composed of women who insisted they did not want or need to vote. They were afraid that political disagreements between husband and wife would ruin marriages. These anti-suffragists argued against state referendums for women's suffrage.

Another factor that created prejudice against the cause of women's suffrage was the alliance between women and the temperance movement. The liquor industry was big business at the turn of the century, and heavy drinking was a social mainstay of all classes of society. The WCTU, which

sought to modify this state of affairs, became particularly active after the Civil War. Therefore, the liquor interests were afraid that women's suffrage would eventually lead to a ban on alcohol. Indeed, this prediction was partially correct, for the Eighteenth Amendment, which banned the manufacture, sale, and transportation of "intoxicating liquors," was ratified after women had attained the vote in some states. But while the WCTU may have contributed to some antisuffrage feeling, it was also a dynamic tool for organizing women.

When Frances Willard was elected to office in the WCTU, she brought her political views—specifically, her support of

WCTU leader Frances Willard's support of women's suffrage centered on the belief that women should have some control over the laws concerning alcohol and drinking.

Widespread Support

Along with the support of the WCTU came the support of the powerful federations of labor: the trade unions. Susan B. Anthony had always supported the labor unions and felt they were a potential source of strength for the suffrage movement. In 1899 the American Federation of Labor, one of the most powerful union groups in the country, voted to officially support women's suffrage. The federation commanded influence with rank-and-file members, both men and women, and its endorsement was a sign that the country was moving toward broad acceptance of women's suffrage.

In this climate of change throughout the United States, the women's suffrage movement began a period of intense activity. Speakers on behalf of the cause went everywhere, crossing and recrossing the nation. At this time, the torch of leadership was passed on to a younger generation of women. When Lucy Stone died in 1893, her daughter, Alice Stone Blackwell, took over her work. The new wave of women who supported suffrage called themselves "suffragists." Leaders included Carrie Chapman Catt, who had joined the movement in 1890, when the two factions of the suffrage movement were reunited.

Essentially a moderate in the Lucy Stone tradition, Carrie Chapman Catt was a tireless organizer who based her strategy for women's suffrage on winning over the states. The West, with its open attitude toward the women of the frontier, was the most fertile ground for state support. In 1894 Catt organized a referendum in Colorado that passed, giving women the vote in that state. The same year, the largest

women's suffrage—into the organization. Willard was a strong public speaker, and she converted many conservative women to the cause of suffrage. Willard's arguments for women's suffrage, of course, emphasized the need to allow women some control over the laws governing drinking; her colorful phrase called for "the mothers and daughters of America [to be able to affect decisions about whether] the door of the rum shop is opened or shut beside their homes."[43] She sent thousands of women across the United States with petitions that included suffrage as well as temperance.

suffrage campaign of the century was organized in California. The California organization raised nineteen thousand dollars, most of it in small donations from working women. The newspapers of the state supported women's suffrage, which would have been unthinkable even forty years before. Susan B. Anthony spoke as often as three times a day, lecturing all over the state.

The difference between the Colorado and the California campaigns was significant, however. Colorado, like Wyoming, was a sparsely populated state at the time, without much electoral power in the national arena. California, in contrast, had both political and economic power. And it had an organized opposition to women's suffrage, mostly in the big business guise of the liquor industry. In fact, the big liquor dealers met in San Francisco to oppose women's suffrage. The Democratic Party also opposed women's suffrage on policy grounds, and the Republicans, yielding to pressure, did not throw full support behind Anthony's cause. The referendum lost in California.

The early successes in passing women's suffrage laws in the states were limited to the less powerful western states. Utah and Idaho joined Wyoming and Colorado, making it legal for women to vote

The suffrage movement gained momentum in the late nineteenth century, thanks in part to such leaders as Alice Stone Blackwell (left) and Carrie Chapman Catt. Blackwell was heavily influenced by her mother, suffragist Lucy Stone. Catt is credited with helping women in Colorado gain the right to vote in 1894.

in 1896. But it would take another decade before the larger and more prominent western states would follow.

The British Suffrage Movement

At the turn of the century, the women's suffrage movement in the United States gained an infusion of energy from the example of the suffrage movement in England, led by Emmeline Pankhurst. Since only an act of Parliament could make

A suffragist is arrested in Great Britain, where demonstrators used radical tactics to draw attention to their cause.

women's suffrage law in Great Britain, British suffragists did not have the option of the gradual states' rights approach; they had to directly convince their national legislature. The British movement used radical tactics: activists went on hunger strikes in prison, handcuffed themselves to posts and railings in public places, and tried every other tactic they could think of to draw attention to their cause. Although like the American movement, the British suffragists could not accomplish their aims until after the First World War, their tactics and flamboyance served as an inspiration to their sisters across the Atlantic, at a time when the American suffrage movement had become quite respectable, if still unable to accomplish its goal.

By 1902 the women's suffrage movement had become international in scope, much in the same way the abolitionist movement had been half a century before. Carrie Chapman Catt served as the president of the International Suffrage Alliance. British suffragists crossed the Atlantic to speak in the United States. Even Emmeline Pankhurst spoke to huge crowds in New York and Boston. American suffragists also traveled to England to observe the political tactics of their sister movement.

At the turn of the century, women's suffrage had gained much wider support than the movement had ever experienced before. This support was due in large part to the changes and growth taking place in the increasingly mobile American society. However, not all factors that contributed to the broader support of women's suffrage came from positive sources. Some support came from those who opposed the recent immigrants from Europe and were distressed by the large numbers of

Views of a British Suffragist

British suffragist Emmeline Pankhurst influenced the American movement. This passage, taken from her autobiography and published in Strong Minded Women and Other Lost Voices from 19th Century England, *shows that her awakening to the situation of women came early in life.*

"My childhood was protected by love and a comfortable home. Yet, while still a very young child, I began instinctively to feel that there was something lacking, even in my own home, some incomplete ideal.

This vague feeling of mine began to shape itself into conviction about the time my brothers and I were sent to school. The education of the English boy, then as now, was considered a much more serious matter than the education of the English boy's sister. My parents, especially my father, discussed the question of my brothers' education as a matter of real importance. My education and that of my sister were scarcely discussed at all. Of course we went to a carefully selected girls' school, but beyond the facts that the head mistress was a gentlewoman and that all the pupils were girls of my own class, nobody seemed concerned. A girl's education at that time seemed to have for its prime object the art of 'making home attractive'—presumably to migratory male relatives. It used to puzzle me to understand why I was under such a particular obligation to make home attractive to my brothers. We were on excellent terms of friendship, but it was never suggested to them as a duty that they make home attractive to me. Why not? Nobody seemed to know."

British suffrage leader Emmeline Pankhurst served as an inspiration to women in her own country and abroad.

African Americans who were leaving the rural South to seek better social and economic opportunities in northern cities.

Chauvinism and the Movement

The immigrants who flooded the cities on the Atlantic seaboard came from eastern and southern Europe. As a result, their customs and languages were distinctly non-Anglo-Saxon and the new arrivals were targets of prejudice from those who wanted to keep the United States racially and ethnically "pure." The immigrants, often politically radical and tending to be associated with labor unions, were looked on by many as radical anarchists. Women's

suffrage suddenly became more acceptable in an effort to prevent these immigrants from gaining political power. Thus some supporters of women's suffrage took the chauvinist position, hoping that strict literacy requirements for voting would disenfranchise immigrants while allowing "white native" women to vote.

The same tactic was used against the African-American community. When requirements for voting were strict, many African Americans would not be able to vote. If white women could vote, white supremacists might have a majority in many southern states. As southern suffragist Belle Kearny said at a 1903 convention, when she also expressed her white supremacist views, "The enfranchisement of women would ensure immediate and durable white supremacy, honestly attained."[44]

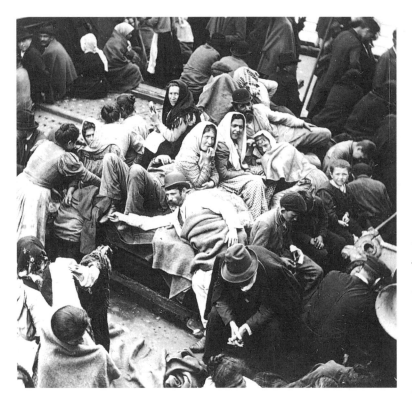

European immigrants huddle for warmth as they wait to disembark at Ellis Island in New York. The women's suffrage movement gained the support of people who hoped that literacy requirements for voting could prevent the flood of immigrants from gaining political power.

Even the National American Woman's Suffrage Association was not above using these racist and chauvinist arguments to further its cause. In an official statement, the association seemed to come out in a backhanded manner for the kind of strict literacy requirements that were used to keep immigrants and African Americans from exercising their franchise:

> Without expressing any opinion on the proper qualifications for voting, we call attention to the significant facts that in every state there are more women who can read and write than the whole number of illiterate male voters; more white women who can read and write than all Negro voters; more American women who can read and write than all foreign voters; so that the enfranchisement of such women would settle the vexed question of rule by illiteracy, whether of home-grown or foreign-born.[45]

Passing of the Old Guard

In this time of accelerated social change, the women's suffrage movement lost its two most powerful original leaders. Elizabeth Cady Stanton died in 1902. And Susan B. Anthony would not live to see the federal amendment for women's suffrage, which was nicknamed the "Susan B. Anthony amendment" in her honor, pass into law. However, Anthony did live to see a far greater acceptance of women's rights in her lifetime. As an enthusiastic audience in Oregon pelted her with roses, she reminded them that fifty years before audiences had thrown eggs at her instead of flowers. On the birthday before she died, Anthony received a telegram of congratulations from President Theodore Roosevelt. Always a fighter for women's rights, Anthony had this reaction: "When will men do something besides extend congratulations? I would rather have President Roosevelt say one word to Congress in favor of amending the Constitution to give women the suffrage than to praise me endlessly."[46]

American society was changing; it was moving away from the stuffy conventions of the nineteenth century, and the status of women would never be the same. However, it would still take some intensive campaigning and a world war before the Nineteenth Amendment would be passed.

7 The Final Push for Women's Suffrage

The First World War both slowed down the suffrage movement and imparted its final impetus. Like the Civil War before it, the First World War caused both men and women to throw their efforts into a patriotic attempt to gain victory and thus to some extent distracted people from the issue of women's suffrage.

The First World War, however, had an effect on women's lives as well as on the suffrage movement. Women took over the industrial jobs left by men who had become soldiers. Women drove trucks, operated freight elevators, ran streetcars, and took over arduous jobs that had been considered the sole province of men. Like the challenges of the Civil War and life on the western frontier, the experience of the First World War gave many women a more competent image of themselves. Granted, when the soldiers came home, women gave up their coveralls and returned to a more domestic sphere, but they never resumed completely their roles of the nineteenth century.

The suffrage movement in the decade of 1910–1920 concentrated on a final push to convince citizens and lawmakers

As men were called away to duty during World War I, women donned overalls and replaced men in many of the industrial jobs previously considered too difficult for females.

Women and Economics

Charlotte Perkins Gilman was a radical feminist thinker and writer. Her book Women and Economics *influenced the women who participated in the final stage of the fight for suffrage. A lecture Gilman gave in 1891 in honor of Susan B. Anthony is excerpted here from Mary A. Hill's book* Charlotte Perkins Gilman.

"And have any of you thought of the personal cost to these early reformers—the women I mean? . . . Now these women—these leaders—these first ones who fought for us so long unthanked—what did they give up? They had to triumph over their woman-hearts and woman-bodies and become human beings; they had to sacrifice in large measure the approbation and kindness of the other sex. Do you think this is a light thing? It is a terrible thing. Do you think they have not felt it? I know they have. Their heads knew they were right and they went ahead, but there were times when their hearts ached for the common woman's need of praise and petting—ached just as yours have ached perhaps and may again. . . . It is always upon the first ones that the worst fate falls. Theirs the unthanked labor, the distrust and scorn, the continual and bitter opposition."

alike that the Anthony amendment should become law. The fight was carried out on two fronts: the effort to win individual states and the effort to pass a federal amendment. These two approaches were closely related. As the states increasingly allowed women to vote, the power of the female electorate continued to grow. And, in turn, this put pressure on the representatives and senators of each state to pass the Anthony amendment.

Final Fight for the States

Carrie Chapman Catt concentrated on suffrage on the state level. In 1910 the western state of Washington granted women the vote. In 1909 Catt organized the Woman Suffrage Party, modeled on the large national Democratic and Republican parties. The goal of the party was to systematically organize the fight for suffrage in large cities, working district by district. Suffrage leaders would target a city and meet with each state senator and local assemblyman. They would distribute leaflets in the streets, give charity balls for the cause, and present the issue of suffrage in every available forum, from school meetings to firemen's parades. Catt emphasized high visibility and propaganda. The Woman Suffrage Party sold buttons and calendars and organized large public parades.

In 1911 California gave women the vote. This was a significant if somewhat

Suffragists campaigned tirelessly in their efforts to promote their message and gain support for their cause.

fraudulent signatures. However, by 1915 Carrie Chapman Catt's organization had brought suffrage referendums to most of the large states, including Ohio and New York. In New York, the suffrage party went all out in its campaign, using the high-visibility tactics of torchlight processions, outdoor events, and even hot-air balloons and Chinese lanterns. All these festivities promoted the cause of women's suffrage. In 1917 the state of New York finally gave suffrage to women. With populous states such as California, Illinois, and New York allowing women to vote, pressure for a federal suffrage amendment increased. For example, if senators or even the president of the United States were elected at least in part by women voters, these office-holders would need to keep their constituents happy—and women voters wanted a federal amendment to continue to guarantee their right to the ballot.

symbolic victory: California was a large West Coast state, but it had far fewer electoral votes than Michigan or Ohio or other more densely populated states. In 1912 Kansas and Oregon passed suffrage laws for women. In 1913 the state of Illinois gave women the right to vote in national presidential elections. This was noteworthy in part because Illinois was the first state east of the Mississippi to allow women to vote.

The fight for the states was not a simple one. Antisuffrage forces sometimes illegally stuffed ballot boxes and succeeded in securing jobs at the polls for sympathizers who deliberately failed to count suffrage votes. The liquor interests fought the suffrage movements with petitions that often proved to have up to 90 percent

Fight on the Federal Level

While Carrie Chapman Catt led the work in the states, Alice Paul was the suffrage leader who concentrated her efforts on the federal movement. Alice Paul had the values of a "New Woman," and she was the only suffrage leader who had not grown up during the Victorian era, the mid- to late-nineteenth century, characterized by the double standard of behavior for men and women. Like many of her predecessors, however, Paul was a well-educated Quaker, and between 1912 and 1918 she took the crusade for a national suffrage amendment into the public eye. Her tactics were partially influenced by the radicalism of Emmeline Pankhurst, with

On the Picket Line

The following is retold from contemporary sources in Olivia Coolidge's Women's Rights: The Suffrage Movement in America, 1848–1920.

"During the First World War, women picketing the White House often were harassed by crowds. When warned about that possibility by the chief of police for the District of Columbia, Alice Paul simply replied, 'The picketing will go on as usual.' The police set up a watch, but suffragists Lucy Burns, Katherine Morey, and Mabel Vernon met in front of the East Gate of the president's residence and pulled out a banner. They set it up and enjoyed several minutes of quiet before one of the policemen happened to turn and catch sight of it.

'The little devils!' he exclaimed. 'Can you beat that?'

The banner contained a simple quotation from President Woodrow Wilson's own words, without any comment. The police were in a quandary. One of them started to make the arrest. Another protested, 'My God, man, you can't arrest that. Them's the president's own words!'

Only after several minutes of indecision did the officers take the suffragists to the police station, where Lucy Burns demanded to know the charge.

'Charge! Charge!' a harassed policeman said. 'We don't know what the charge is yet. We'll telephone you that later.'"

Alice Paul learned many of her radical tactics from British suffragists like Emmeline Pankhurst. One of her most effective tactics was having women picket the White House.

whom Paul had been arrested in a British demonstration.

One of Paul's tactics was to have delegations of women picket the White House directly. Even in the rain, they stood outside the gates, holding banners that proclaimed, "Mr. President, What Will You Do For Woman Suffrage?"[47] Paul was playing to the press as well as to the White House. She had special days for picketing—days for different states, for teachers, for labor unions, and even for Susan B. Anthony's birthday. During the war, the women picketers who stood outside the White House were heckled as traitors. Yet the suffragists took President Woodrow Wilson's war message of fighting for democracy and the ideals of the U.S. Constitution to heart and emblazoned it on a banner as further proof of the right of women to vote: "We Shall Fight For The Things Which We Have Always Carried Nearest Our Hearts—For Democracy, For The Right Of Those Who Submit To Authority To Have A Voice In Their Government."[48] During the war, Alice Paul was arrested and sentenced to seven months in jail. Her hunger strike kept women's suffrage in the limelight. These radical tactics of civil disobedience brought the cause of women's suffrage even more strongly before the public.

Paul's tactics included the staging of enormous marches and demonstrations in favor of women's suffrage. One of the largest was planned for the day before Wilson's inauguration in 1913. Five thousand women set off to march down Pennsylvania Avenue. Police protection was insufficient, there was heckling from the crowd, and, perhaps not surprisingly, a riot soon broke out between the pro- and antisuf-

Suffragists from across the country prepare to march on Washington in 1913. With over five thousand participants, the parade drew national attention.

frage contingents of spectators. But Alice Paul's goal had been met—the issue of suffrage had gained national prominence. Also, the issue of suffrage was brought dramatically to the attention of the president. Suffrage parades remained a tactic until the passage of the Nineteenth Amendment. In 1914 Paul founded her own suffrage association, named the Woman's Party, to carry out her campaigns.

While Carrie Chapman Catt concentrated on suffrage on the state level, Alice Paul continued with her high-visibility approach to bringing home a federal amendment. The double effort is what eventually won the suffrage cause. Both tactics had the same underlying power—women, whether as voters or as marchers, represented political pressure on the U.S. Senate, the body that could translate women's suffrage into law.

For the Anthony amendment to become law, it had to be approved by a two-thirds majority in the Senate and a two-thirds majority in the House of Representatives. Women won the House in a state-by-state fight. As states granted the right to vote to women so did their representatives in the House. The amendment had first been proposed to the U.S. Senate in 1878, but it was rejected that same year. It was defeated again in 1887. In 1914 the suffragists presented the Senate with a petition of five hundred thousand signatures, asking that the Anthony amendment become law. Once again, the Senate voted no. However, in the suffragist campaign of 1918–1919, the Senate was won over.

The Democratic and Republican national committees had come out in favor of the amendment. The support of the national parties was a reflection of the attitude of the American population at large.

Under increasing pressure, President Wilson publicly announced his support of the Anthony amendment in 1918.

Seventy-five years of social change for women had finally made women's suffrage seem not only just but necessary. And of course both Democrats and Republicans hoped to benefit from the women voters allied to their respective parties.

Most important, President Wilson announced his support of the amendment. The First World War was almost over, and Wilson's attention was turned from winning the war to establishing peace. On the international front, Russia had given women the vote, and Germany was about to do so. Canadian women could vote; British women had been promised the vote after the war was over. It was increasingly embarrassing for Wilson to represent democracy in the world forum when the leaders of all the other nations knew that the United States did not allow women to vote. In 1918 he made a public statement to women suffragists of the Democratic Party: "I am, as I think you know, heartily in sympathy with you. I have endeavored to assist you in every way in my power, and I shall continue to do so. I shall do all I can to assist the passage of the Amendment by an early vote."[49] The day after Wilson's declaration of support, the amendment passed the House of Representatives. In June 1919 the Senate also approved the amendment. However, for the amendment to pass into law, the suffragists needed the approval of thirty-six states. In a well-organized campaign, Carrie Chapman Catt began the last push for suffrage in the states. Tennessee became the thirty-sixth state to approve the amendment.

On August 26, 1920, the Nineteenth Amendment to the Constitution was ratified, guaranteeing suffrage to all women in the United States. In the fall of 1920, women were finally able to register to vote in national elections. Millions went to the polls.

Olivia Coolidge, a historian of the women's suffrage movement, later noted:

It was seventy-two years since Elizabeth Stanton's original meeting in Seneca Falls, women had conducted fifty-six referenda campaigns, four hundred eighty campaigns to get states legislatures to submit suffrage amendments to voters, forty-seven campaigns to get state constitutional conventions to write woman suffrage into state constitutions, two hundred seventy-seven campaigns to induce state party conventions to include woman suffrage into state constitutions, two hundred seventy conventions do to likewise, and campaigns—some nominal but some intensive—in nineteen successive Congresses.[50]

When the Anthony amendment was won, Carrie Chapman Catt proposed that the National American suffrage organization become the League of Women Vot-

The Nineteenth Amendment

The Nineteenth Amendment to the U.S. Constitution gave women the right to vote. This amendment was proposed on June 4, 1919, and became law on August 18, 1920.

"Amendment 19:

Section 1. The right of citizens of the United States to vote shall not be denied or abridged by the United States or by any State on account of sex. [Neither the United States nor any state has the right to keep a citizen from voting because she is a woman.]

Section 2. Congress shall have power to enforce this article by appropriate legislation. [Congress has the power to make laws that will make this amendment effective.]"

Alice Paul and other members of the National Woman's Party cheer the passage of the Nineteenth Amendment.

ers. The first order of business for the new group was to help women vote. Techniques included lining up election day baby-sitters and transportation to the polls for women who wanted to vote. The league gave demonstrations on how to mark a voting ballot and campaigned to simplify voter registration in the states. Today, one of the main functions of the League of Women Voters is to publish useful election leaflets that outline the positions of candidates.

Just as the Fifteenth Amendment did not make specific provisions for women, the Nineteenth made no explicit mention of black women. For African-American women, the road to suffrage did not end with the passage of the Anthony amendment. Throughout the South, it was difficult for African-American women to register to vote. They were forced to wait in line until white women had registered,

sometimes as long as twelve hours. Some southern states harassed would-be voters by giving African-American women literacy tests and requiring proof of taxpayer status and property ownership. These requirements were imposed selectively on African-American women.

African-American women brought a statement to the National Woman's Party, which continued to exist after the passage of the Nineteenth Amendment as a focus of support for women's rights. This statement read:

> We have come here as members of various organizations and from different sections, representing five million colored women of this country. We are deeply appreciative . . . of the tremendous sacrifice made under your leadership in securing the passage of the Nineteenth Amendment. . . .

[Black women] have also come today to call your attention to the flagrant violations of the intent and purposes of the Susan B. Anthony Amendment in the elections of 1920. . . .

We cannot . . . believe that you will permit this Amendment to be so distorted in its interpretation that it shall lose its full power and effectiveness. Five million women in the United States cannot be denied their rights without all the women of the United States feeling the effect of that denial. No women are free until all women are free.[51]

The National Woman's Party failed to offer a meaningful response to the concerns of its African-American supporters. Thus for African-American women within the suffragist movement, discrimination would continue on the basis of race. It was not until the civil rights battles of the 1950s and 1960s, when voter registration

drives in the South put an end to many abuses of the system, that the Anthony amendment was interpreted to secure the rights of African-American women as well as Caucasian women.

The suffrage movement in the United States accomplished its goal in part by focusing on the vote as a single issue. The women's rights movement envisioned by Mott and Stanton had taken a larger view of woman's place in society and sought to improve it. Some of these other goals had been won as well. By the early twentieth century, women were able to attend college and to train for the professions, although not in the same numbers as men. Both married and single women could own property and control their earnings. Even dress reform had been accomplished, and by the 1920s, women wore short haircuts, less encumbering skirts, and, eventually, pants. The ideal of equal pay for equal work remained unrealized, however, and there were still many social

A League of Women Voters registration campaign in action. At its inception, the League's primary goal was to help women exercise their right to vote.

In 1963 thousands of people march to the capitol in Washington D.C. demanding greater civil rights for African Americans. The civil rights battles of the 1960s helped end discriminatory practices that prevented many black women from voting.

constraints on a woman's life. These issues would erupt forty years after women gained the vote in what can be considered the "second wave" of the women's rights movement in America: the feminist movement of the 1960s and 1970s.

However, the suffrage movement had indeed achieved its stated purpose. Although Susan B. Anthony did not live to see the ratification of the amendment that bore her name, the slogan she lived by had been upheld: "Failure Is Impossible."

Feminism: The Aftermath of the Suffrage Movement

The suffrage movement created higher expectations for women. In the years after the passage of the Nineteenth Amendment, American women continued to make social and political gains. The Second World War, like the First, brought a change in the status of women. Women worked as welders, operated drill presses, and cut patterns for airplane parts. Women also served in the military.

In the postwar years, women did return to more traditional roles, concentrating on home and family life. But the suffrage movement's demands for equal pay for women and equal rights in the so-cial and political spheres did not die out. In the early 1960s, a new women's movement began in the United States. This second wave was called the feminist movement. It had as a theoretical basis the work of Betty Friedan, author of *The Feminine Mystique,* and the French philosopher Simone de Beauvoir, who wrote *The Second Sex,* which attacks the oppression of women on all fronts, including their roles in the male-dominated family. Just as the early proponents of suffrage had been influenced by the writings of Mary Wollstonecraft, so de Beauvoir influenced a movement across the Atlantic.

While women have made enormous strides in the last century, discrimination on the basis of sex still exists. This continuing discrimination has prompted the fight for passage of an Equal Rights Amendment. Here, marchers carry a banner with the wording of the proposed amendment.

The New Feminism

The goals of the feminist movement included opening the professions to women, who were underrepresented in the fields of medicine, law, and engineering. It included a demand for equal pay for equal work, because, as a rule, women were paid less than men to perform duties having the same job description. The feminist movement also addressed the issue of men and women sharing child care and housework. And it attacked the assumptions of a society in which rape and other forms of violence against women were commonplace.

The feminist movement was an outgrowth of the suffrage movement and a continuation of the idea of women achieving full equality. This second movement was necessary because the right to vote and the guarantee of protection under the law did not suffice to allow American women to be fully equal. The early suffrage leaders, particularly Elizabeth Cady Stanton, were well aware that women's equality could not simply be legislated; the hearts and minds of both men and women had to change so that women could be regarded as full human beings.

The second wave of feminism did indeed meet some of its goals. In particular, middle-class women began to enter the professions in larger numbers and to have careers in business and academia. The women's liberation movement became organized, in the form of the National Organization for Women, and had its own media publications, the most successful of which was *Ms.* magazine, founded by Gloria Steinem.

Like the suffrage movement, the feminist movement has its detractors as well. Antifeminists, such as public speaker Phyllis Schlafly, calls feminist demands "anti-family, anti-children, and pro-abortion . . . a series of sharp-tongued, high-pitched, whining complaints by unmarried women." She continues, "Women's lib is a total assault on the role of the American woman as wife and mother, and on the family as the basic unit of society."[52]

A Look to the Future

The second wave of feminism helped bring women more freedom, but like the suffrage movement, it often neglected to include the concerns of minority and non-middle-class women. Its gains can be seen in the lives of women who have satisfying work outside the home, as well as economic and political power. Its continuing challenge can be found in the observation that still, on the average, women earn less than men.

Both the suffrage movement and feminism grew out of other reform movements. Both began with a broad range of issues that eventually narrowed, into suffrage and the proposed Equal Rights Amendment. And both movements could concur with Elizabeth Cady Stanton, "But it still requires courage to question . . . the position of women."[53]

Notes

Introduction: Women and the Ballot

1.   Quoted in R. Conrad Stein, *The Story of the Nineteenth Amendment*. Chicago: Childrens Press, 1982.

Chapter 1: Women and the Abolitionist Movement

2.   Sarah Moore Grimké, "Reply to the Pastoral Letter," quoted in Miriam Gurko, *The Ladies of Seneca Falls: The Birth of the Women's Rights Movement*. New York: MacMillan, 1974.

3.   Mary Wollstonecraft, *A Vindication of the Rights of Woman*, quoted in Gurko, *The Ladies of Seneca Falls*.

4.   Quoted in Sara M. Evans, *Born for Liberty: A History of Women in America*. New York: Free Press, 1989.

5.   Elizabeth Cady Stanton, *Eighty Years and More*. 1898. Reprint, Boston: Northeastern University Press, 1993.

6.   Stanton, *Eighty Years and More*, quoted in Elizabeth Griffith, *In Her Own Right: The Life of Elizabeth Cady Stanton*. New York: Oxford University Press, 1984.

7.   Stanton, *Eighty Years and More*.

8.   Quoted in Griffith, *In Her Own Right: The Life of Elizabeth Cady Stanton*.

Chapter 2: The Convention for Women's Rights at Seneca Falls

9.   Lucretia Mott, "Discourse," quoted in Gurko, *The Ladies of Seneca Falls*.

10.   Stanton, *Eighty Years and More*.

11.   Stanton, *Eighty Years and More*.

12.   Stanton, *Eighty Years and More*.

13.   Quoted in Gurko, *The Ladies of Seneca Falls*.

14.   Quoted in Gurko, *The Ladies of Seneca Falls*.

15.   Stanton, *Eighty Years and More*.

16.   Quoted in Olivia Coolidge, *Women's Rights: The Suffrage Movement in America, 1848–1920*. New York: E. P. Dutton, 1966.

Chapter 3: Susan B. Anthony and the Women's Movement of the 1850s

17.   Quoted in Susan Clinton, *The Story of Susan B. Anthony*. Chicago: Childrens Press, 1986.

18.   Stanton, *Eighty Years and More*.

19.   Quoted in Gurko, *The Ladies of Seneca Falls*.

20.   Quoted in Gurko, *The Ladies of Seneca Falls*.

21.   Quoted in Gurko, *The Ladies of Seneca Falls*.

22.   Quoted in Coolidge, *Women's Rights*.

23.   Quoted in Griffith, *In Her Own Right*.

24.   Quoted in Evans, *Born for Liberty*.

25.   Quoted in Evans, *Born for Liberty*.

Chapter 4: The Civil War and the Passage of the Civil Rights Amendments

26.   Quoted in Stein, *The Story of the Nineteenth Amendment*.

27.   Stanton, *Eighty Years and More*.

28.   Quoted in Gurko, *The Ladies of Seneca Falls*.

29.   Stanton, *Eighty Years and More*.

30.   Quoted in Paula Giddings, *When and Where I Enter: The Impact of Black Women on Race and Sex in America*. New York: William Morrow, 1984.

31.   Quoted in Giddings, *When and Where I Enter*.

32.   Quoted in Giddings, *When and Where I Enter*.

33.   Quoted in Giddings, *When and Where I Enter*.

34. Quoted in Giddings, *When and Where I Enter.*

35. Quoted in Giddings, *When and Where I Enter.*

36. Quoted in Giddings, *When and Where I Enter.*

37. Lucy Stone, quoted in Gurko, *The Ladies of Seneca Falls.*

Chapter 5: The Changing Role of Women

38. Stanton, *Eighty Years and More.*

39. Stanton, *Eighty Years and More.*

40. Quoted in Evans, *Born for Liberty.*

Chapter 6: Changes at the Turn of the Century

41. Quoted in Stein, *The Story of the Nineteenth Amendment.*

42. Quoted in Stein, *The Story of the Nineteenth Amendment.*

43. Quoted in Evans, *Born for Liberty.*

44. Quoted in Evans, *Born for Liberty.*

45. Quoted in Evans, *Born for Liberty.*

46. Quoted in Stein, *The Story of the Nineteenth Amendment.*

Chapter 7: The Final Push for Women's Suffrage

47. Quoted in Stein, *The Story of the Nineteenth Amendment.*

48. Quoted in Stein, *The Story of the Nineteenth Amendment.*

49. Quoted in Coolidge, *Women's Rights.*

50. Coolidge, *Women's Rights.*

51. Quoted in Giddings, *When and Where I Enter.*

Epilogue: Feminism: The Aftermath of the Suffrage Movement

52. Quoted in Evans, *Born for Liberty.*

53. Stanton, *Eighty Years and More.*

For Further Reading

Susan Clinton, *The Story of Susan B. Anthony*. Chicago: Childrens Press, 1986. A short account of the life of women's suffrage leader Susan B. Anthony. The book includes details of her work in both the temperance and suffrage movements.

Sara M. Evans, *Born For Liberty*. New York: Free Press, 1989. A broad overview of women's role and social history in the United States from colonial times to the present. *Born For Liberty* looks at social movements from union organizing to dress reform.

Doris Faber, *Oh, Lizzie! The Life of Elizabeth Cady Stanton*. New York: Lothro, Lee and Shepard, 1972. A delightful account of the life of Elizabeth Cady Stanton written for young readers. While it is historically accurate in its details, it is also entertaining and readable.

Paula Giddings, *When and Where I Enter: The Impact of Black Women on Race and Sex in America*. New York: William Morrow, 1984. A comprehensive examination of the role of African-American women throughout American history, including their lives under slavery and within the suffrage movement. The volume includes numerous hard-to-find primary source materials.

Miriam Gurko, *The Ladies of Seneca Falls: The Birth of the Woman's Rights Movement*. New York: MacMillan, 1974. One of the best compilations of factual account and primary source materials about the birth of the women's rights movement in the United States. Written in a readable style, it contains both individual biographies of important women leaders and an overview of the subject.

R. Conrad Stein, *The Story of the Nineteenth Amendment*. Chicago: Childrens Press, 1982. A simple and straightforward account of the historical events that were necessary for the Nineteenth Amendment to become law. An informative and easy-to-read book.

Additional Works Consulted

Olivia Coolidge, *Women's Rights: The Suffrage Movement in America, 1848-1920.* New York: E. P. Dutton, 1966. A chronology of the women's suffrage movement. Emphasizes contemporary views of historical events, and is particularly strong on the period from 1890 until the passage of the Nineteenth Amendment.

Frederick Douglass, *Narrative of the Life of Frederick Douglass, An American Slave.* Edited by Benjamin Quarles. Cambridge, MA: Harvard University Press, 1971. The original account by reformer Frederick Douglass that charts his life as a slave and his escape from slavery.

Hannah Duggan, "The Women's Rights Movement in the United States," unpublished paper, 1994. A term paper written by a seventh grader in Newark, Delaware, using some of the reference books in this bibliography.

Don E. Febronbacker, editor, *Abraham Lincoln: Speeches, Letters, Miscellaneous Writings.* New York: The Library of America, 1989. A compilation of writings of Abraham Lincoln. All primary source material.

Christiane Fischer, *Let Them Speak For Themselves: Women in the American West, 1849–1900.* Hamden, CT: Archon Books, 1977. An excellent compendium of eyewitness accounts of how women lived on America's frontier.

Elizabeth Griffith, *In Her Own Right: The Life of Elizabeth Cady Stanton.* New York: Oxford University Press, 1984. A comprehensive biography of this leader and thinker of the women's rights movement. Includes discussion of her early life through her reform years through the writing of a *Woman's Bible.*

Mary A. Hill, *Charlotte Perkins Gilman.* Philadelphia: Temple University Press, 1980. A biography of the first major woman economist in the United States. Gilman was a thinker and writer associated with the early twentieth-century women's movement.

Corinne K. Hoexter, *Frederick Douglass: Black Crusader.* Chicago: Rand McNally, 1970. A biography of the man who went from slavery to life as a reformer. Frederick Douglass was an early supporter of universal women's suffrage.

Janet Murray, *Strong Minded Women and Other Lost Voices from 19th Century England.* New York: Pantheon Books, 1982. A varied and fascinating collection of primary source material. Includes firsthand accounts of girls' boarding schools, women's dress, anti-suffrage sentiment, and domestic economy.

Abbey Slater, *In Search of Margaret Fuller.* New York: Delacorte Press, 1978. A look at the life of transcendentalist thinker and writer Margaret Fuller. She did not live to see an organized women's movement, but influenced it with her writing.

Elizabeth Cady Stanton, *Eighty Years and More.* Boston: Northeastern University Press, 1993. Elizabeth Cady Stanton's lively account of her own life is one of the best primary sources available on the women's suffrage movement. Stanton writes about her girlhood and her life as a leader of the women's movement.

William St. Clair, *The Godwins and the Shelleys: A Biography of a Family.* New York: W. W. Norton, 1989. An extensive look at Mary Wollstonecraft's family, including husband and philosopher Godwin, and daughter Mary, who married the poet Shelley.

Mason Wade, *Margaret Fuller.* New York: The Viking Press, 1940. The life of Margaret Fuller.

Mary Wollstonecraft, *A Vindication of the Rights of Woman.* New York: W. W. Norton, 1967. The important philosophical work on the rights of women that inspired the leaders of the women's suffrage movement in America, such as Lucretia Mott. The first feminist book written in English.

Index

Oregon, women's suffrage in, 76
Pankhurst, Emmeline, 70, 71, 76-78
Panton, Jane Ellen, 40
Paul, Alice, 76-79
Philadelphia Female Anti-Slavery Society, 14
Phillips, Wendell, 47
property rights, for women, 24, 34, 58
organizing to get, 11, 28, 36-38
public speaking
of Anthony, 61, 62
by women
ban against, 34, 52
increasing, 15, 65
as right denied, 29, 32
women's movement and, 52-53, 68

Quakers, 14, 16, 33

racism. *See* discrimination
registration, voting, 10-11, 81-82
Republican Party
in suffrage campaigns, 53, 69
women's support for, 45, 47
Rollins, Lottie, 51
Roosevelt, Theodore, 73
Ruffin, Josephine St. Pierre, 49

Schlafly, Phyllis, 85
Sewell, Sarah, 25
slavery, 44
see also abolition movement
Stanton, Elizabeth Cady,

19-22, 25-26, 43-45, 73
teamwork with Anthony, 35-36, 38, 42
women's rights and, 23-24, 36-41, 67
Declaration of Sentiments and Resolutions by, 28-30
planning for Woman's Rights Convention, 22, 26-28
in women's suffrage movement, 60-61
politics of, 47, 50-51, 53, 63
Stanton, Henry, 19, 21, 25-26, 29
states, women's suffrage in, 65, 66
federal government and, 56, 74-76, 79
western, 57-60, 68-70
Steinem, Gloria, 85
Stone, Lucy, 32, 52-53, 68
Sumner, Charles, 47

temperance movement, 33-35, 52-53
effect on women's suffrage movement, 11, 65, 67-68
Thirteenth Amendment, 45
Truth, Sojourner, 42, 47-48

Utah, women's suffrage in, 69

violence, against women, 85
vote, right to, 10-11
for African Americans,

18, 45-46, 47
effects of, 34, 85
see also women's suffrage, campaigns for the vote

wages
equality in, 58, 85
inequality in, 62, 82
Washington, women's suffrage in, 75
Wells-Barnett, Ida, 51-52
West, the, 68-70
White House, 77-78
Willard, Frances, 67-68
Wilson, Woodrow
pickets at the White House and, 77, 78
support for Nineteenth Amendment, 79-80
Wollstonecraft, Mary, 17, 18
Woman's Party, 79
Women's Rights Convention in Seneca Falls, 29-31, 32
planning for, 22, 26-28
Woman Suffrage Party, 75-76
women, 43
against equal treatment, 25, 66-67, 85
images of, 64, 74, 85
of woman's place, 25, 30, 53, 54-55
oppression of, 13, 16-17, 20
in Declaration of Sentiments and Resolutions, 28-29
social life of, 17, 54-55
see also education; jobs, women's; vote, right to

Picture Credits

Cover photo: UPI/Bettmann

The Bettmann Archive, 16 (both), 17, 19, 21, 23, 26, 31 (bottom), 38, 39 (bottom), 43, 54, 65

The Kansas State Historical Society, Topeka, 57

Library of Congress, 10, 12, 13, 14, 20, 24, 27, 29, 31 (top), 33, 34, 36, 39 (top), 40, 41, 44, 45, 52, 55, 56, 58, 60, 62, 63, 66, 68, 69 (right), 70, 71, 72, 76, 77, 78, 79, 82, 83

National Archives, 30, 74

Stock Montage, Inc., 49, 53, 81

UPI/Bettmann, 48, 51, 64, 69 (left)

Copyright Washington Post; Reprinted by permission of the D.C. Public Library, 84

About the Author

Miriam Sagan holds a B.A. in English from Harvard University and an M.A. in writing from Boston University. Her books include *Tracing Our Jewish Roots* from John Muir Publishers, as well as numerous collections of fiction and poetry. Her work has also appeared in such magazines as *Ms., New Mexico Magazine, American Book Review, Family Circle, Mademoiselle,* and the *Christian Science Monitor.*

PROPERTY OF:
KENTLAKE HIGH SCHOOL LIBRARY